THE LITERATURE OF
DEATH AND DYING

THE LITERATURE OF DEATH AND DYING

Advisory Editor
Robert Kastenbaum

Editorial Board
Gordon Geddes
Gerald J. Gruman
Michael Andrew Simpson

In After Days

THOUGHTS ON THE FUTURE LIFE

BY

W. D. HOWELLS, HENRY JAMES, JOHN
BIGELOW, THOMAS WENTWORTH
HIGGINSON, HENRY M. ALDEN
WILLIAM HANNA THOMSON
GUGLIELMO FERRERO
JULIA WARD HOWE
ELIZABETH STUART
PHELPS

ARNO PRESS

A New York Times Company

New York / 1977

Reprint Edition 1977 by Arno Press Inc.

Reprinted from a copy in
   The University of Illinois Library

THE LITERATURE OF DEATH AND DYING
ISBN for complete set: 0-405-09550-3
See last pages of this volume for titles.

Manufactured in the United States of America

------◆------

Library of Congress Cataloging in Publication Data
Main entry under title:

In after days.

      (The Literature of death and dying)
      Reprint of the ed. published by Harper, New York.
      1. Future life--Addresses, essays, lectures.
I. Howells, William Dean, 1837-1920. II. Series.
BT899.I5 1977   236'.2   76-19576
ISBN 0-405-09574-0

In After Days

WILLIAM DEAN HOWELLS

In After Days

THOUGHTS ON THE FUTURE LIFE

BY

W. D. HOWELLS, HENRY JAMES, JOHN
BIGELOW, THOMAS WENTWORTH
HIGGINSON, HENRY M. ALDEN
WILLIAM HANNA THOMSON
GUGLIELMO FERRERO
JULIA WARD HOWE
ELIZABETH STUART
PHELPS

WITH PORTRAITS

HARPER & BROTHERS PUBLISHERS
NEW YORK AND LONDON
MCMX

Contents

Illustrations

In after days when grasses high
O'er-top the stone where I shall lie,
Though ill or well the world adjust
My slender claim to honored dust,
I shall not question or reply.

I shall not see the morning sky;
I shall not hear the night-wind sigh;
I shall be mute, as all men must
In after days!

But yet, now living, fain were I
That some one then should testify,
Saying—"He held his pen in trust
To Art, not serving shame or lust."
Will none?—Then let my memory die
In after days!

—From "Poems on Several Occasions," by Austin Dobson.

A Counsel of Consolation

William Dean Howells

In After Days

I

A Counsel of Consolation

NOTHING you can say from your thinking will avail with the newly bereaved,
but anything you say from your knowing
and believing and feeling will be precious.
They want your pity, your compassion, your
sympathy; and though there never was a
death which did not seem to accumulate upon the mourners incidents of peculiar anguish, yet if you can match these
from your own experience they will be hum-
bly grateful. Some chance word of yours,
the least considered or directed, shall find
them in their sorrow and help them beyond
your utmost hope. In our doubt of this we

3

shrink from trying to help, lest we rather hurt, but I think there could not be a greater mistake. Nature, which includes death as maternally as birth, has within it the yearning for companionship in grief as in joy. For the bereaved the world has been emptied of what seems to have been the supreme good, and the void aches for any form of kindness with which friendship can help fill it.

I keep saying the same thing differently over to justify myself in offering a suggestion which will shock the witnesses of sorrow rather than the sorrowers themselves. My prime counsel to these would be to trust not only to eternity, but also to time, for consolation, and to trust time first, for time is here and now, and eternity is hence and of the future. This counsel does not imply forgetting; to grief, which is of love, that is impossible; but it is well to realize from the universal human experience that the agony of to-morrow will not be the agony of to-day; the sharpness will have been dulled a little, and a morrow will come when the lacerating edge will be rounded so that you shall not feel it except as a stress that will no longer tear your heart, and then no stress, but a valued consciousness. You shall even wish to feel it; there will be a sweetness in it which you would not forego, but would keep with you for life.

I cannot truly speak to the stricken from the absolute faith which some others can speak from. I am of those who patiently wait for the fulfilment of the hopes which Christianity has worded from the Greek philosophers rather than from the Hebrew prophets. Once I asked my father, a man whose whole life was informally but deeply religious, whether he kept the vivid interest in his doctrine which he once had. He was an old man, and he answered me, "Youth is the time to believe, age is the time to trust." Now I am myself an old man, and more than ever I feel the wisdom of this saying. There are many things that I doubt, but few that I deny; where I cannot believe, there I often trust; and as all faith is mystical, I would have the bereaved trust their mystical experiences for much truth which they cannot affirm. In their darkness it will

5

be strange if there are no gleams of that outer light which wraps our whole ignorance of this life. These will penetrate it sometimes in what seem preternatural experiences of the waking hours, and sometimes in visions of the night, which I would have the sorrower at least passively accept, or not positively refuse. Others can say that such visions, such dreams, are figments of the overwrought brain, but no one whose despair they have brightened will reject them. Whether they are natural or supernatural, they are precious; whether they are the effect of causes quite within ourselves, or are intimations to us from the source of all life that death too shall have an end somewhere, somehow, they are to be cherished and kept in the heart, and not cast out of it as idle and futile. They may be the kaleidoscopic adjustment of our jarred and shattered being; they may be prismal rays of celestial light: who shall say from knowledge? What they oftenest involve is that reunion with the absent which the whole soul yearns and grieves for. Once more, while they last, we have our lost again; we clasp them and hold

6

them to our hearts; we talk with them, face to face, and they tell us—

"What and where they be."

When such dreams fade they leave us not so all disconsolate, and while their glamour lasts our darkened world is illumined from their radiant world. So it seems, and their glamour shall never wholly pass unless we will it, and misprize them. If we speak of them too freely they dim sooner; the effort to fix them in words is fatal to them, but if we keep them hushed in the secret of our abiding sorrow when it is no longer agony, they will remain a lasting comfort. In the hour of "sharpest pathos," I would say: Seek the help that offers itself to your seeking from those sources of healing which all the generations of Christianity have known. Go to your Bible, which, perhaps from your long estrangement, will have grown newly potent and significant; go to Plato for the converse which Socrates held with his weeping disciples when in the face of death he hailed the eternal life; go to the nobler poets, or to any poet in his nobler mood. It is not

7

at random that I speak here of Tennyson's *Two Voices* and certain passages of *In Memoriam.* The very look and sound of the words had healing in them. I do not say that they were of the same quality of comfort as the affirmations of unquestioning faith; but often in the hour of grief the fabric of religion, which the whole of life has built up, crashes into the dust of death, which in its turn seems to resume the whole of life. I am speaking mainly to those whom this ruin befalls, and who cannot accept the assurance of others' faith. These cannot dwell even upon the words of divine or apostolic promise and continue to find in them the hope and assurance which they once gave. Then nature must trust to nature, to dreams and visions, to the exalted poems, and take what comfort it can in them.

Nature encompasses otherwise the whole of being, and she brings the anodyne, the narcotic, the nepenthe, in which the bereft are presently reprieved of their agony. The house of mourning is in these transports the house of mirth; the time to weep is also the time to laugh. Amid their sobs a wild gayety suddenly bursts from the mourners as if it burst upon them; it passes, and then the burdened heart relieves itself again in tears. I would not have the mourners strive to repress these outbursts, as something unworthy and unfit. They are the effect of nature offering escape from otherwise intolerable pain, and beginning in the very presence of death the consolation which time will complete. Often they come through the uninvited remembrance of something quaint or droll in the character of the dead, and so far from involving slight or irreverence they imply the share of the absent in the transport of that moment for which the living deny death. For that moment the dead are with us again in the fond and familiar intimacy of custom not then sensibly broken forever; they are more tenderly dear because they seem to return among us in the intimacy of love and home.

These reliefs I urge the more because they are from within ourselves, and I would not have any one reject them, the most mystical of them, for the reason that they are from within us. If "the light is within you," it is not the light for your guidance alone, but the light for your solace also. For those whose faith is broken by the blow dealt, or is weak from long disuse, here is comfort from which it would be folly to turn. Doubtless the supreme comfort can come, waiting the effect of time, only from the authority of revelation, by the mouth of the priest, or by the mouth of some strongly believing friend. It will not matter what church the priest is of, it will not matter how poor and ignorant and humble the friend is; it is enough if either be sincere. There is help for the bereaved from the church, perhaps because the church has been the help of so many in so many ages; it is strengthened for its office by the beaten and broken helplessness of the myriads who have turned sorrowing to it; their tears and cries have consecrated it as they have consecrated the written Word. But so is there help from the living faith incarnate in some believer who takes the groping hand in the strong grasp of his confident trust and leads the way.

There is relief, there is help, there is even hope in the testimony, which will come from

all sides, to the kindnesses that the dead did
when living, and I would have the mourners
give the freest access to this testimony. It
will have been a life so hard and sterile as
to be all but impossible if some deed of
beneficence has not fallen from it in its way
through the world, and such a life there will
be few or none to grieve for when it is extinct. All other lives will have left the remembrance of good actions forgotten by the
doer, but not forgotten by those they were
done to. These will gladly come with their
remembrance, and there can be nothing
sweeter to the sorrowing than such a proof
that their dead are worthy of their grief.
If there is to their grief any high or any
humble, as indeed there should not be, in a
time rapt from the world and the pride of
life, then the last shall be first with them,
and the lowliest whom their lost one has
made his friend shall be the welcomest. No
such friend should be kept from them by a
foolish decorum; he has a right to tell them,
and it is the right of the dead that he should
tell them of the goodness he has experienced.

I suppose that we have all sometimes

shrunk from speaking or writing a word of
compassion to the mourners in the house of
death, but this is from a false and mistaken
forbearance, I think. We know that we shall
write inadequately, awkwardly, foolishly, perhaps; but we ought to know that the gratitude of the bereaved will supply our defects.
They wish to dwell upon every aspect of his
vanished life in the sight of those who knew
him, or only saw him, even. They instinctively long to keep his "loved idea" before
their eyes as it is reflected in the eyes of
others, and I believe those would err who
should try to distract them from their grief,
at least in the first days of it. Let them
abandon themselves to it; do not seek to
part them from it; if any chance does so,
they will feel lifelong that they have not
grieved their heartbreak out, that they have
somehow been robbed of the sorrow which
is one of the most precious experiences of
love. Again, in all this, there is something
mystical, and we cannot follow anguish in
the ways by which it best assuages itself.

I would have those who grieve keep close
and fast every association with the dead;

soon enough such memories will pale and fade away. I would have them think of the faults of those who are gone, the foibles, the frailties, which in every human being help to make up his sum, and endear him equally with his virtues. If there is a world beyond this, these will go with him to it, and become the stuff of his regeneration and redemption. I would have the mourners recall hours of gladness, of merriment, spent with the dead, and live over with them in a joyous comradery, joyous, if only for a fleeting instant, the times which time cannot bring again. It may be that there is—

"Nessun maggior dolore
Che il ricordarsi del tempo felice
Nella miseria."

But though it is—

"Truth the poet sings
That a sorrow's crown of sorrows is remembering happier things,"

yet if we empty memory of all but the gloomy and piteous experiences of the past we invite despair and madness. It *is* a great

anguish to recall the happy time in wretch-
edness, but it is also a great help, a great
defence. Except rarely, except improbably,
sorrow does not kill, for sorrow is something
nobler than mere brooding upon irreparable
loss; that indeed may kill, or, worse yet,
craze. Sorrow is patient, sorrow is even
cheerful, and willing to give itself to the
trouble, the affliction of others. It is eager
to share another grief in which it will lose
itself, and if there is a counsel of consolation
which I would offer above all the rest to the
mourner it would be to seek out in the very
ecstasy of pathos some instance of affliction
and minister to it.

Religion will help, reason will help, love
will help, but only time will truly bring relief. It will seem a hard saying, in the black
hour from which there is no visible issue, to
declare from the universal human experience
that there will yet be the full light of the
common day in the house of mourning; it
will seem profanation, almost, it will seem
sacrilege. Yet it is true; and the light of
the common day is the very light of heaven.
The time will come when you shall not in-

deed forget your dead, but when they shall be helpfully, not hurtfully, with you. The passion, the wild, headlong, hopeless passion for reunion with them, will have resolved itself into a patience in which they will always be present, and responsive to your thought, which, whenever it strays from your work or your play, will seem to find them quietly grateful for it. You will not forget. You may no longer see the mystical beauty, the sublimity of the dead face, but out of the farther past the living eyes will look, and now and then, among the myriad faces, infinitely unlike one another, there will chance a face from which an evanescent semblance will flash a radiance into the place where her face, his face, is in your heart and restore it to your vision.

Is it a freak of fleeting fancy, is it an effect of the eternal truth? "Tell us, tell us," sorrow implores, "shall we see that face again, and see it always? If a man die, shall he live again?" There is no answer in science or experience, only the voice of One who taught as if with authority, "If it were not so I would have told you."

I would have the mourners grieve all their

sorrow out, and not stay from dwelling on
their loss; without fully realizing this, they
cannot begin to retrieve it. "Keep before
you," I would conjure them, "the vision of
the face, the form, you shall see no more on
earth, and let it pass only of itself, hoping,
longing for its return when it fades away.
But do not frame this image from the memories of the dead in their hours of sickness,
or even in the hours after pain when they take
on the majesty and beauty of eternal peace.
Those hours are but as instants in the long
tale of the years that went before. Return
in your tenderness, turn again in your despair, to the records of those happier years,
and reconstruct from them the truer likeness
of your beloved. See him gay and glad, full
of life and purpose, of work and play, of jest
and earnest, such as he veritably was, and
do not wrong him by the presentment of his
suffering or its mortal surcease. Make him
your own again, by putting this out of your
thoughts, and inviting into them the semblance of him when his life was the habit of
your own, and he was most himself in some
fortunate, some joyous moment."

ELIZABETH STUART PHELPS

The Great Hope

Elizabeth Stuart Phelps

II

The Great Hope

"THE setting of a great hope is like the setting of the sun."

The familiar words of one who was acquainted with grief, and who held its solemn charter of expression, recur to you as an event hitherto unmet. Your own event has transposed as it has transformed every other. Feeling and fact pass under the most relentless autocracy in the world—the government of sorrow. You know your first great bereavement.

To say that it stuns you is to use the only verb that expresses the opening effect of your personal tragedy. Many of the words which anguish has chosen for its outcry from the beginning of pain to the end of peace cannot be replaced. We may chafe under their familiarity, and call them time-worn, but we can never call them time-dishonored. The most averse of us will find them on our lips, or in our hearts, in the great crises of life. This is one of such words. You are stunned, we say, by what has befallen you. At first, you do not even ache under it. Your subterranean consciousness perceives the fact, but of its relation to your capacity for suffering you know, at the beginning, no more than you do of the literature of Mars.

The instinct of all hurt animals is much the same. You crawl to some mercifully desolate spot. As the key snaps in your door a deeply imbedded nerve in you seems to start with it. This is the nerve of the conscious pang.

Outside the window there is silent space. There are hills and sky. There is light, and the diminution of light, and the formation of shadow in places where light was. Stupidly semi-conscious of familiar outlines, and yielding to the eternal human impulse to seek the horizon, you turn half-blind eyes to the gleaming west. The sun is going down. Color masses against color, like tints never seen before upon a shrinking palette. You do not recognize the familiar, daily incident. It whirls before you like the movement of earthquake or volcano or flood—something unnatural and incredible; there is a moment when it seems to be preposterous. This is followed by a sense of fear which, it occurs to you, will in some form last forever. The sun has dipped, has dwindled, has blurred, has swung into a solemn twilight, has plunged to an impenetrable night—the first upon a new-closed grave. Into this strait and narrow darkness you enter as your dead has entered—you are almost as separate, you are almost as alone. At first you are still. For a time you are as cold.

Sensation returns not like that after paralysis, tingling slowly, but like that after certain concussions, with sudden smart. All the aching forces of the universe seem to have crashed upon you. It is as if you had become the central nerve of pain. The hapless self-concentration of a first grief possesses you; nor, in the healthier conditions of a slowly acquired peace will you recall it with anything but honest pity, such as you would feel for another's woe or error, or for inexperience in any form. Time teaches. The recurring seasons lift. The daily routine sustains. "The hours are too strong for you." A sane philosophy—or even a live religion, if you are so fortunate as to have one—comes to your relief, if not altogether to your rescue. When you have found that you *can* bear your misery as the rest of the race have borne theirs before you—when you discover that you need not curse God and die, because your personal happiness is counted out of the system of things—then you are ready to confront your fate and ask it questions. If these are the questions of the rack to the inquisition, call them by their dark names; for nothing is gained by ignoring the first blasphemies of grief. Admit them, if they exist. Endure, if so it be, as vigorously as you suffer. Writhe, since you must. Curse, if you would. Anything is better than a paralytic despair. Be true, even to your manias, in the process of healing. Sanity never comes of self-deception. It comes of candor, as much as it comes of struggle. The unreason of a great grief

passes into the mental health of acceptance
by a beautiful and subtle process in which
God and the soul work together—the soul
never knowing how, but conscious sometime,
in some way, in part or in full, of a Power
not itself, that makes for comfort.

I know of but two things in the experience
of a real bereavement which cannot be borne;
and I do not hesitate to say that it is asking
too much of any sensitive human spirit to
demand that they should be borne—at least,
without the throes and blows of a rebellion
which may be as creditable to a broken heart
as what we call resignation; or may, in fact,
in the end, lead to that strong condition
which we are apt to dismiss from our respect
as a pious and feeble fallacy; until we ourselves have experienced it.

He is a fortunate mourner who finds his
sorrow unhaunted by spectres darker than
itself. Remorse is the one worst, the one
intolerable element in affliction. Blessed beyond his own knowledge is he who finds himself companioned only by gentle memories of
his dead: he to whom the acutest pangs pos-

sible to grief are strangers: he whose love for the living, like the love of the New Testament definition, was "kind," while it had the opportunity.

There is no more pitiable being in the world than a man who, really loving, or really believing that he loved, yet inflicted upon the living—perhaps in the fire of anger, or perhaps in the froth of thoughtlessness—that for which he cannot ask the pardon of the dead. The hurt may have been slight, if you choose to call it so, but it takes on a mortal character in the retrospect. There was a duel of natures or a war of words; there was an hour stained with red which has dyed the memory through and through; they who loved became as they who hated—and wounds slashed where caresses had been; and perhaps the dead forget, but the living, God pity him! remembers.

The slow surprise of dear incredulous eyes; the sudden shocked sense of inconceivable pain—the mute reproach—the silence more surcharged than any outcry—these return and recur like the films in a limited and monotonous biograph. The memory sits bound hand and foot before moments which a man would give his life to forget. But, in proportion as he is a man, he does not forget.

It does not matter very much that he may not have been altogether to blame, that his friend was, or was believed to be partly at fault, for now the only thing he does forget is that the loved and vanished was ever in the wrong. It is not the faults of the dead that we recall; it is our own. It is not our own lovable traits that we dwell upon; but theirs. "I have come to think of you," said an aging man to a friend, "as never forgetting, and always forgiving." It is good to be given words like these while we can hear them. For the hour comes when there is nothing left for us to do but listen; when the whole being becomes one exquisite ear, like the curved body of Burne-Jones' Eurydice in hell, entreating the eternal silence for articulation which does not come. The powerful and discordant Carlyle will be remembered no longer for his great history than he will be for his cry over the grave of the wife whose life he bruised while he had her:

"Blind and deaf that we are: oh, think,

if thou yet love anybody living, wait not till
Death sweeps down the paltry dust-clouds,
and idle dissonances of the moment."

"Oh, why do we *delay* so much till Death
makes it impossible?"

"Oh, my Dearest, my Dearest, that cannot now know how dear!"

Of all the thrilling incidents told us by the
evangelist who moved Boston last winter, one
will longest pursue us.

A Maine fisherman lost his little girl in a
fog. He left the child upon an island rock
while he went to fish, and, fishing, forgot her.
The tide was rising. With the tide came the
fog. When at last he found his way back to
the spot where he had left the little thing she
had been swept away. To this day it is said
that the disordered father reiterates these
hapless words:

"If I had only stayed where I could hear
her cry!"

Piteous the truth, but, like all truths, to
be faced! The fogs of life crawl subtly between those who love, and tides rise, and
waves drown while we are having a pleasant
time, and capable of forgetting. Then we

row back—desperately, out of our reckoning, and calling all the way. A little remembering, a little fidelity, a little steadiness or kindness would have made the dreadful difference. Perhaps it is better to know this too late than never to know it at all; but in the bitter education of life there can be no crueler knowledge. If I had only stayed near enough to hear her cry! . . . If I had only kept close enough to hear him call! These are the self-reproaches which no self-delusion can silence. Nothing is so hard to bear as that which could have been prevented.

After our first bereavement, who dares any longer drift beyond the range of drowning cries? In an utter sense, at a solemn cost, we learn to stand by those we love.

It would be a waste of the emotional force to dwell upon the element of remorse in bereavement, if it did not carry its own consoling quality with it—and this, I think, in a peculiar way it does. Nothing is so sure as that love forgives. Although we love, we may hurt. In proportion as we are beloved, we shall be forgiven. What if we did harass him to the quick for whom we mourn? What if we did wound her to the death for whom we grieve? In all the world of life or death, he would be the first—she would be the swiftest—to forget. It may be well "to have it out" with our haunted memories once for all, and trust the dearest dead, as we should have trusted the dear living to comfort us for the very wrong that we wrought upon themselves.

It may be that no one else can do this. It may be that no one else would. He will, whose life you damaged. She will, whose heart you broke. Love will, because it is love. There is no such thing as an unforgiving spirit, if that spirit loves. Death does not make our beloved less trustworthy, less tender, or less true. Who shall say that the process of passing from this life to the other does not make them more so? In their way, they may develop under the separation as much as we do. In their consciousness, as in our own, the energies of love may intensify through parting. It is impossible to put a limit to the power of the dead—or the will of the dead—to forget that they were ever grieved or harmed.

One of the supreme passages in all literature is De Quincey's apostrophe to the Bishop of Beauvais, who sentenced Joan of Arc. Ever since, a child in my father's study, I first heard him read it while I sat listening "with a wild surmise," the words have illuminated for me, like no others outside of Holy Writ, the nature of forgiveness; perhaps the nature of a living and therefore growing spirit:

"My lord, have you no counsel? 'Counsel I have none; in heaven above, or on earth beneath, counsellor there is none now that would take a brief from *me*.' . . . Who is that cometh from Domrémey? . . . who is she that cometh with blackened flesh from walking the furnaces of Rouen? This is she, the shepherd girl, counsellor that had none for herself, whom I choose, bishop, for yours. She it is, I engage, that shall take my lord's brief. She it is, bishop, that would plead for you; yes, bishop, *she*—when heaven and earth are silent."

The only other unbearable thing that I know in the endurance of bereavement is the apparent finality of it. Any temporary separation between the living can be borne. Which soul of us is not man enough to accept our share of the universal doom, if it is not to be a permanent one? Who could not spare his beloved patiently, if he must, for a little while? Who could not wait for the touch of the vanished hand if, in the width of the spaces or the gulfs of the mysteries, it is groping anywhere for ours? He was right whose half-inspired, half-narcotized vision selected the sound of "everlasting farewells" as the epitome of human despair. Love claims in proportion to its intensity, and all genuine love defies the grave as a man fighting for his life defies his assailant. I incline to go so far as to say that, if we do not clasp our dead again beyond the barriers of their mystical silence, it is our own fault.

It all comes, in the end, perhaps, to a matter of feeling—profound and high-minded feeling. The intellectual argument for personal immortality is quite strong enough to cover the case. But it may not be supple enough, and the case may outrun it. By as much as love is greater than reason, there

remains · the larger argument for the everlasting life. There are souls born doubters,
as there are bodies born cripples, and there
will always be a certain proportion of minds
to which the sublimest promise of the Christian faith is not *sympatica*, and therefore not
comprehensible. One may look upon skeptics
of the sneering and irremediable type as
spiritual defectives. Honest they may be—
pitiable they certainly are. One would go
any length of sympathy with their misfort-
une; but one cannot mistake deformity for
health and beauty. Unbelief is not an enviable thing; there is nothing grand or noble
about it. Nothing can be more erroneous
than to take it as a sign of intellectual superiority. This is a common mistake of
those who are either half-read, or *half-felt*
in the study of spiritual questions.

It is probable that there have been more
words written to prove or disprove the doctrine of personal immortality than have cen-
tred upon any other subject of human
thought—it is certain that there has been
more thought expended upon it. Probably

all intelligent people have their own favorite method of approaching the question. To my own mind the intellectual argument— not philosophically, but simply speaking— may be summed in some such form as this:

Life is a consequence, looking for a cause. The Creator is either a system of things or an individual force. In any case, He has eventuated in a world of individuals. These feel, on the whole, more than they think, and suffer, on the whole, more than they enjoy.

The preponderance of misery over happiness in the human race is so tragic that it constitutes the darkest mystery of creation. There is no solution of this mystery except in some form of reimbursement to the suffering. (This may not be theological, but it is logical, and I am not at all afraid to say it.) The creating force is either good or evil, kind or cruel, and must act accordingly. The hypothesis of a malevolent Deity is intellectually perfectly coherent; but morally it is so monstrous that it must be counted out of any cursory consideration like this. If we are in the control of benevolent power, we are entitled to expect benevolent treatment. If God is good, He will be kind.

If God is kind, He could not make a world of woe like this one, and stop there—it is not that He would not, or should not—He *could* not. It would be the *reductio ad absurdam* of philosophy. It is perfectly conceivable that He might create a suffering world, for beneficent ends of His own, partly apparent even to us, even now and here— but only partly apparent. It is as inconceivable that He should pack this planet with the agonies that it holds, if these are the beginning and end of the story, as it is that He should permit the sins and manias of the race, if there is never to be given an opportunity to evolve into moral sanity.

One may say it with reverence none the less profound for the courage of the words, that the character of Godhead itself is on trial in the history of this unfortunate world. Life is scarcely more than an experiment in vivisection, if death is the end of personality.

Personality exists in proportion to power, and, of all personal forces, love, in this system of things, is the supreme agent. It is not sufficiently understood that love is its own god; capable of deciding for itself the question of immortality. As a man feels, so he is. As we love, so we are to be. It is to an appalling or a blessed extent for you to decree the nature of your future. If you love greatly, if you love utterly, if you love nobly— what power in the universe can decide that your love shall cease to be? I can conceive of none. It rests with yourself whether you shall love so highly that no low, material accident, like physical death, can slay your love. As long as love lives, it has the claims of an energy upon its source. It is easy for us to perceive that God is power. It is a slow lesson for us to understand that God is love. Perhaps it took the Christian Scriptures to give us the splendid epigram.

Love, for most of us in this life, is at once a sad and glorious thing. We come to the brow of the grave with a little struggling shape of human happiness in our arms, and drop it there—buried alive. Still warm, breathing yet, palpitating to our lips, it slips under the earth, and cries after us as it slides away: "I have not died. Save me! Save me, that I live again!"

Too often, it should be remembered, we are the slayers of our own buried feeling. He who cannot love strongly, he who cannot love steadily, may live beyond death—we do not say that weak feeling, like weak thought, may not have its fair chance—but he who does not love sufficiently to insist upon another life, if only for love's sake, may have missed his ablest advocate for personal immortality.

Fidelity is the most uncertain of human traits. In this, dogs, are clearly the superiors of men. The terrier to whom a monument is erected in Scotland because he slept upon his master's grave every night, in all weathers, for twelve years, surpassed most mourners of the master race, in loyalty and in grief. If great and permanent love is, in itself, a prophecy of immortality—I anticipate the question—yes. The dog deserved another life, and I have no personal difficulty in supposing that he may have it, if any of us do.

In the background of all thoughtful souls lurks one question which most of us evade, but which none of us escape. The weakness of human feeling, the uncertain power to hold ourselves to "the highest when we see it," is not so apparent or so perplexing in any other relation as in that between man and woman. Marriage is an attempt to fix this relation in its noblest form: but a noble spirit may fail in realizing the endeavor. The man who has loved his living wife devotedly may recoin the gold of feeling, "no matter whose the print, image, and superscription once" it "bore." Human loneliness is the most inexorable power this side of death, and all but the royal allegiances go down before it. In youth we are severe upon this affectional errancy. All young lovers believe in the eternity of love—their own, and that of others. In middle life and age we grow tolerant of far feebler weakness than that involved in the temporal quality of affection. Many a man's heart has ached its way through the experience of love and ties not his first, without coming to any ease in the direction of a future life. The perplexity is too fine for him— perhaps too sad. Fine it will always be, and sad it must remain. What is to become of

the cross-currents of feeling in the world to
be? How adjust, in the new life, relations
that are unadjustable here? Where shall we
put the later love? How shall we face the
old? What is there to be expected but an
emotional and even an intellectual confusion
which may deprive what we call heaven of
one of its chief elements of peace or even
comfort?

Only one thing seems to me possible to *say*
—whatever we may think or feel—upon this
matter. When we consider the adaptability
of our affections here, we may infer something of their amenability to unknown conditions hereafter. We love, or think we love;
yet we love, or think we love again. Nevertheless, there must exist the supreme feeling,
or the composite ideal of feelings. Who shall
gather this blossom of being? And how
shall it be sown and grown? Jesus Christ
spoke a wonderful and mystical word upon
this matter. Pondering upon it, as every
one must who has speculated much upon the
future life, I have come to this conclusion:
When we consider what time does for us,
what growth does for us, what character does,

and experience, in this world—it is not necessary to fret ourselves about the affectional
dénouements of the next.

Take the single fact of human friendship.
What capacities in it! What evolutions from
it! What revelations, what atonements, what
prophecies! He who has found a friend, or
proved one, may be for that reason farther
on the way toward the life everlasting than
he supposes.

But he who loves nobly and is nobly beloved has stepped already across the invisible and magical border. Who knows but
that love in another world may partake of
some of the firmer qualities of friendship in
this one? While still it may not lose its
own essence, exquisite and ineffable, its wan-
dering soul which goes clamoring here for
immortality like an orphaned child for a
home.

But the mourner at the new grave does
not concern himself with the impermanence
of human feeling. He is not troubled lest
he should cease to love. He is busied only
with trying to bear his power of loving. Yes-

terday, to-day, and forever, his need of his dead seems to him the supreme fact of life. As he kneels in the grass to plant flowers above dust too precious to be neglected, he is planting solemn and exacting hopes in his nature; these have deep roots, and, like other rooted things, they will blossom if they are cherished.

Because he loves and grieves, he believes in the life everlasting—and, so long as he loves, and believes, he has reason to expect it. Somewhere, somehow—his idea of the where or the how is vague, but so is mist, and like amber mist at the setting of a slant sun, this clings to him—at some time, and for some reason, he dreams that he shall clasp the dear dead thing that he has laid away. Let him dream, and bless God that he can.

If it were but a vision of the darkness, who would awaken him? For there is no fact on this earth so actual as that dream. There is no argument so powerful as that hope. There is no philosophy so blessed as that belief. Nay, more than this—I would rather believe that I should find my lost and loved again, and be mistaken about it, if that were possible, than to believe that the grave were the end of hope and faith, of happiness and comfort, of love and loyalty; and then learn, after all, that these precious things would live as long as I live, and last as long as I love; and that the spirits of my dead would turn to me in the end, the patient, hurt faces of the loving and the slighted. Whether it be a truth or a soul, that which we value must be cherished to be held.

Love (as I have elsewhere said, if I may be allowed to say again) is not a sketch, but a serial story; it runs on past this life "to be continued" in the next; or else there should have been no story at all. Better to live and die blank and bleak of heart, than to experience the ecstasies and agonies of any real affection, and stand quivering to see death cut the chapters off midway and forever. The Author of the greatest tale told in all the universe is an Artist; and He will complete His work. This is our reasonable hope, and, if it were not, we who live by it, and would die for it, are of all men most miserable. Possessing it, we should be, of all, the happiest.

If death is treated as an incident—separation as an episode—reunion as a prospect—grief can be borne as a momentary interruption to an eternal joy.

JOHN   BIGELOW

Is There
Existence After Death?

John Bigelow

III

Is There Existence After Death?

A LAWYER would naturally say, in answer to this question, that the burden of proof lies upon those who deny the continuity of life. He might then ask what the contestant means by Death. If told, "the change undergone when our soul or spirit is separated from our bodies," as we are bound to presume he would, he may fairly be answered that such separation no more signifies a termination of life than the falling of the leaves in winter connotes the death of the trees. The material body is only a transitory abode of Life; no more Life itself than the garments with which we clothe it; than a stove crammed with burning coals is any part of the heat which the coals assist in generating and the stove in radiating.

All the constituents of a man on this planet are Material or Spiritual; what of us is not material is spiritual, and what is not spiritual is material. But matter has no element or attribute capable either of producing or of maintaining life. Though some motion of all the atoms of all matter is a consequence or incident of every variation of temperature; though this variation is incessant; though chemical and polar variation is also incessant; though the diurnal and annual motions of the earth are perpetually changing the position of every atom of our planet—yet no atom or multiple of atoms has a power of its own either to initiate or to suspend motion. Hence matter cannot be fatigued. If it could be, it could and would waste, shrink in bulk, and finally perish. But the scales of the chemist have effectually disposed of the delusions so long entertained of the destructibility of matter. The conception of its diminution or annihilation is now as absurd as would be the conception of its birth from nothing.

When, therefore, what is commonly called Death separates the Soul from Body, Spirit from Matter, and "this corruptible puts on incorruption," matter does not part with a single attribute or quality necessary to its perpetuity or integrity. It continues as before to undergo changes in obedience to forces which do not belong to it and over which it has no control whatever. It continues incapable of diminishing or of increasing itself, whatever may be the process or force to which it may be subjected.

In parting with my body, therefore, I shall merely have parted with a transient implement as destitute of life as a spade or a plough, or Franklin's kite, by which he dragged the lightning from the heavens, though not a spark of the lightning was in the kite itself.

As the matter of which our body is composed is without any initiative; utterly lifeless; does not die; cannot be killed; cannot even diminish;—where is the life of which the body was for so long a faithful and obedient servant, it being no longer a part or tenant of the body? It must be somewhere.

It cannot have gone with the body into loam, for loam, of course, has no more life than the body from which it is dissolved. As the Life never was a part of the loam, and therefore could not have gone with the body into loam, it must be presumed to be, what it was before the separation, a spiritual substance or entity, and to have passed on into the state or existence in which enfranchised spirits must be presumed to have been gathered from time immemorial.

II

Man's incarnation was necessary to qualify him to profit by the educational opportunities of what we call his earthly life and environment. But as in this our earthly environment or kindergarten, our children are left by the parents at school only for so long a time as they think may prove most advantageous to them, so are we detained by or discharged from our carnal bonds when we have received from them all that we are likely to receive to our advantage, or perhaps also when temptations greater than we might prove able to successfully contend with threaten us.

But such separated Life is not visible to the natural eyes of the terrestrial man. Neither is it ever actually visible to him in the flesh. The natural eye only sees in any man what is spiritual in him as reflected from his features, gestures, language, and behavior. These, however, are all only spiritual impressions, as purely such even while in the flesh as they will be when separated from it, however much more accurate they may be presumed to become when the observed shall be relieved from the many worldly temptations to appear other than what they are. Everything we love and everything we hate, every virtue and every vice, is spiritual and only spiritual. Every man may become more or less charitable or selfish, liberal or avaricious, loyal or treacherous, just or unjust, but neither the one nor the other has ever been or can ever become more or less than the precise spiritual quantities their names imply. Whenever we undertake to describe another person, the only characteristics that we remember and feel are those which when reduced to their ultimate ratio inspire us with more or less of esteem or of the reverse, —all purely spiritual impressions. Hence the Christian, in what is known as the Dominical prayer, does not say to God, "Be Thou hallowed," which would seem most natural, but "Hallowed be Thy Name" (and all through the Bible, praise and service are offered to God's name, not directly to Him), for the obvious reason that it would be a mockery to pray for the sanctification of the Infinite, whom we can never hope fully to comprehend, and of whose attributes our estimates are liable to change every year— nay, every day—of our lives. We can only pray without profanity that the Name, which represents to each of us only what he actually does know or thinks he knows of God, may be sanctified or hallowed, that and nothing more. The Name changes to our eyes in value in perfect correspondence with the increase or the decrease of our knowledge of God. So it does also with that of all our fellow-creatures. Hence, however devout we may be, it is possible that, though the Almighty

is unchangeable, we may never pray twice
to precisely the same God.

III

All of life consists of what we love and of
what we do not love. There are no hopes,
aspirations, ambitions, or interests animat-
ing the heart of man which do not resolve
themselves into one or both of these cate-
gories. Whatever, therefore, we do is done
in obedience to our Will, which represents
what we most love or do not love, or what we
are compelled by circumstances for the time
being to most love or not love. Yet both
Love and Will are purely spiritual causes.
Whatever is done at their behest by the incarnate man are only effects. Matter, the
slave of man, we have seen, is itself immortal. Could anything be more preposterous than to assume that this Master
dies at the grave and the Slave lives on forever?

But it may be said that matter is immortal
only as matter and on this planet or planets

like this. How does it follow that the Spirit which has deserted its containment, or has been deserted by it, has survived?

The proper answer to this question is simply to state what that Spirit loved or hated. Do we love any or all of what are commonly regarded as virtues—temperance, patience, truth, justice, benevolence, charity, modesty, humility—or do we more affect the opposites of some or all of these virtues? If either, they are our life and they are all spiritual. As none of these virtues or their opposite vices can ever be less virtues and vices, of course, therefore, they are immortal. All of us may become more or less temperate, charitable, humble, or truthful, but temperance, charity, humility, and truthfulness can never become more or less virtues.

Once, some fifty years ago, I woke from a deep sleep with so fresh a recollection of a dream, the quality of which had never before entered my mind so far as I could recollect, and which was so vivid that I was able when I arose to go to my library and record it in my diary. It is not inappropriate, I think, to insert here:

"The human mind can conceive of no time when $2+2$ began to be 4 or will cease to be 4. It never could have been nor can it ever be otherwise.

"God is infinite truth. The above result is necessarily a part of God, because it is a necessary part of infinite truth. To suppose a power of denying that $2+2$ make 4 is to suppose a power of denying all truth, which is not supposable."

In other words, God is a state or Composition of all the qualities necessary to perfection, and which, like a mathematical axiom, never could be more or less at any time.

IV

There are several other questions which should be answered before there will be any occasion for the believer in a future existence to take the witness-stand.

Ours is the only species of the animal kingdom that is never satisfied with what at any moment it is, has been, or has done. Its

successes are regarded practically as but steps
to a higher plane. We are always struggling
to accumulate power; whether in the form
of health, of strength, of knowledge, of experience, of skill, of wealth, of popular esteem or influence. The passion to better
our state or position, to accumulate more of
something that we value, is an emotion which
distinguishes us more than any other species
of the animal kingdom, and animates us to
the very close of our earthly life. To this
passion Shakespeare puts into the mouth of
Hamlet this masterly expression:

> "What is a man
> If his chief good and market of his time
> Be but to sleep and feed? A beast, no more.
> Sure, he that made us with such large dis-
>   course,
> Looking before and after, gave us not
> That capability and godlike reason
> To fust in us unused. Now, whether it be
> Bestial oblivion, or some craven scruple
> Of thinking too precisely on the event,
> A thought which, quarter'd, hath but one part
>   wisdom
> And ever three parts coward, I do not know

Why yet I live to say, 'This thing's to do';
Sith I have cause and will and strength and
   means
To do't. Examples gross as earth exhort me."

What pretext or excuse can be made for the creation of a planet—not to say an incalculable number of planets—and stocking ours with creatures whose environment is specially calculated to fit them to become purer, wiser, and better than they ever do become while incarnate, and yet who are always impelled by desires which result in more or less successful struggles to become purer, wiser, better, or in some way, at least in their own eyes, more important? Surely such a life, if terminating at the grave, can only be regarded as but a fragment, as only a page of the great volume of a human life, as only the atrium of one of God's noblest temples. What possible reason can be assigned for even suspecting that this trend of development should not go on indefinitely, only far more rapidly when separated as it would be from what was never a part of it, what shall have ceased to be even a convenience to it, and threatens to become an obstruction only avoided by a separation from it?

V

During the last century physical science made marvellous contributions to man's power over previously latent forces in nature. One of not the least significant consequences has been to give the captains of industry wealth, rank, and social position such as they had never before enjoyed in any age, in strange contrast with their position when Plato denounced the study of mathematics as beneath the dignity of a philosopher. From the bench of their newly acquired social eminence these scientists have rashly proclaimed that the wise man could accept nothing as true but what could be demonstrated by the unaided human reason. The natural corollary of this dogma is that what the scientists do not know is unworthy of belief. However, it exactly suits that enormous proportion of the human family which worship idols made with hands. It also naturally inspires them with profound respect for the scientist who gives the highest possible sublunary sanction of their worship of idols of silver and gold. What better authority was needed than such fashionable Rationalists as Tyndall, Herbert Spencer, and Wallace to countenance the worship of this world for what there is in it; in putting the Bible away on the upper shelves of the library as "mere literature"; in leaving the Church to such victims of superstition as were not sufficiently enlightened to see the absurdity of its pretensions to a divine origin, and devoting their Sabbaths to automobile excursions, to games of ball, tennis, or bridge; and finally to the conversion of all churches into lecture-rooms or music-halls? They now had not only scientific but fashionable authority for saying, "Prove to me by inexorable logic that there is a God, that He inspired the Bible, that there is a life beyond the grave, and prove it by the same inexorable logic as Newton proved the attraction of gravitation, then, perhaps, I will believe in your God, frequent His temple, respect His Sabbath, and prepare myself for your imaginary future life.

Till then you can expect nothing of the kind from reasonable creatures."

It never occurs to any of these short-sighted Pharisees, wise as they fancy themselves to be, that none of their scientific authorities, however eminent, has ever been able to demonstrate the absolute truth of any one of the sciences they profess, or has ever reached the frontiers of any science whatever.

Sir Isaac Newton enjoys the reputation of having discovered a law which controls the greatest amount of power or force of which the scientist pretends to have any conception. The tradition is that while resting under an apple-tree in his garden an apple fell upon his head. In searching for the reason why the apple had fallen, and why others, becoming detached from the tree, fell also to the ground, while none of them fell upward or sideways, he wisely concluded that they must have obeyed some superior force that made them fall to a lower level rather than in other directions. Lacking knowledge of the real cause of this propensity of apples as well as of most other things unsupported to descend, he named the force they obeyed *Attraction of Gravitation*, a phrase or title which had no more meaning than the X Y Z of an algebraic formula. If it signified anything more than a "sound and fury," it stood in his equation as the representative of some power of which he only knew that it makes things unsupported fall to the level of a lower support.

Newton had yet to learn that man can only know what *has happened and its derivates*, but never knows, only conjectures, what may happen from what has happened. Newton presumed from what he had observed of the habits of apples and other things, that all material things would continue to fall unless supported. This presumption from the orderliness of nature was not science, but Faith. All causes imply the exercise of some Will and all Will is spiritual. All causes, therefore, are spiritual and have to be inferred by the scientist from their resulting phenomena. The experience of every creature is illustrated in the answer which Moses received when he said to our Creator,

"I pray Thee, if I have found grace in

5

Thy sight, show me now Thy ways *that I
may know Thee."* The Lord replied:

"Thou canst not see My face: for man
shall not *see Me and live.* Behold, there is a
place by Me, and thou shalt stand upon the
rock: and it shall come to pass, while My
glory passeth by, that I will put thee in a
cleft of the rock, and will cover thee with
My hand until I have passed by: and I will
take away Mine hand: and thou shalt see
My back: but My face shall not be seen."

In other words, our Creator, the *Causa
Causans* (the Supreme Will), is a spirit and
cannot be seen by man while in a state of
nature—that is, while in the bonds of the
flesh. As the Cause of Causes, the Active in
every phenomenon, is spiritual, Moses could
see it only after it had passed: in other words,
by results. He saw only its back, as the scientist sees phenomena and from them in-
fers their Causes as best he can. HE SEES
THE REAL OR FINAL CAUSE OF NOTHING.
Only the infinite can see or be seen by the
infinite.

The Baron of Verulam was a great philosopher, and as such he is justly famous, but

his fame as a philosopher rests entirely upon the popularization of the lesson to which we have referred, and which Moses received while in the cleft of the rock on the Mount, thousands of years ago. Bacon taught men to infer as much as they could of the laws of their Creator from facts observed, from events that had occurred, instead of trying to infer facts from imaginary laws and jejune presumptions. He taught the scientist to search for wisdom and observation from the results evolved by experiment and observation and to trust no conclusions about the Creator's work adopted *before the Creator had passed by.*

The results of the Science of the Rationalist at best are but hypotheses, the possible fragments of a truth, but in no sense absolute truth. They are vessels of which any man may drink, but none of them are like Joseph's "cup, with which he divineth." We infer that the sun that disappears this evening will reappear the following morning, but that is not the conclusion, but only an inference of science. The inference that the sun will reappear to-morrow is Faith, without which the scientist is as blind as the beast that perisheth, for neither can demonstrate the truth of what is not. That can be rendered even probable only by Faith, which, as the Apostle Paul, with scientific accuracy, said to the Hebrews, "is the assurance of things hoped for; the proving of things not seen. For therein the elders had witness borne to them. By faith we understand that the worlds have been framed by the Word of God, so that what is seen hath not been made out of things which do appear."

But Faith is not material, but spiritual, and what advantageth it a man to know what has been, without the faculty of trusting at discretion upon the consecutive relations of events and the probable consequences?

In what respect, then, ought our faith in sunshine to-morrow to differ from our faith in the continuity of life after parting with its earthly garments? We cannot demonstrate, neither can we deny either, while for both there is every probability and for neither any demonstrable improbability.

VI

It is the manifest purpose, end, or function of the scientist to search for and disclose the mysteries of the earth he inhabits and depends upon for his subsistence. As his disclosure of these mysteries increases, what is more natural than that his dominion over spiritual forces should also be more abundantly disclosed to or by him, *pari passu* ? All nations and tribes, whether civilized or savage, recognize in their fellows as virtues charity, honesty, generosity, temperance, patience, diligence in one's calling, obedience to legitimate authority, courage in doing what we think right and just. All these qualities without exception are such as contribute to happiness in this world, and are all parts of every religion, whether Christian or Gentile. The veriest thief, liar, reprobate, or outcast of whatever shade, expects *from others* nothing more or better than each and all of those virtues and many others. He respects every one who has them, and denounces their absence from every one but himself. But every one of those qualities and every one of their opposites are spiritual. In dropping or shedding his material garments he experiences no substantial change or privation. He remains precisely the same man after his heart has ceased to beat as before. He has experienced no change but the removal of the checks to his spontaneity. He may now gratify all his dominant desires, appetites, and wishes without the prompt penalties of excess against which, in his earthly life, he was wont to be providentially warned. As he has parted at the grave with nothing which constituted any part or quality of his life, his course of life is not even interrupted. On the contrary, he is presumably far more alive than ever, as his will is emancipated from all earthly restrictions to its gratification.

These are all logical presumptions from all his earthly experience. To suppose that his life, therefore, terminates at the grave would be not a particle less absurd than to infer from a frost in December that your garden would never yield strawberries again. Hence every Rationalist professes to have less faith than every gardener may be presumed actually to possess.

In After Days

Who ever experienced a sudden and overwhelming calamity, threatening death or even insupportable humiliation, that did not look up to the power that has been proving itself so much greater than his own, without an instantaneous appeal to it for mercy or help? It is to him a sudden revelation of his impotent subordination to a power incalculably superior to his own. When, during our Civil War, the North had a million of men in the field warring with another army only a little less numerous, no one old enough to have been a concerned observer of those times but must have noticed how largely the press, the literature, and the platform eloquence of that crisis reflected a sense of even greater dependence upon the goodness and mercy of supernal authority than upon the bravery of our soldiers, the skill of our generals, or the wisdom of our statesmen. Lincoln, in his Gettysburg address, only voiced the Spiritual elevation of the nation because of its trials, as the ebbing and flowing of the ocean tides respond to the revolutions of the moon.

Deplorable and unprecedented as have been the recent dispensations of Providence in the south of Italy, the reports which are coming to us not only from there, but from other sympathetic nations, render it not difficult to believe the assurance they give to not only the Italian survivors, but to the rest of the world, that there is a God that rules, and that man was not created in His or in any image, merely for what he was or could become during his brief incarnate life. It is not so much through our blessings as through our trials, our sufferings, and our disappointments, that we feel both the need and the certainty of a God of Love that controls our destinies; that what He creates is never born to die. Cowper, in describing the great Sicilian earthquake of 1783, says:

"Revelry, and dance, and show
Suffer a syncope and solemn pause,
While God performs upon the trembling stage
Of His own works His dreadful part alone. . . .
His wrath is busy and His frown is fell."

Nothing produces upon us a more spiritualizing influence than imminent danger.

Hence the sailor is one of the most superstitious of wage-earners—that is, one of the most religious—according to his lights. It is proverbial that one who goes to sea never knows where he will be buried. The more the sailor learns of the treachery of the sea the more he puts faith in the Ruler of the Seas and in that Ruler's love and mercy. He faces its most imminent perils with the same composure as any ordinary professional duty.

The least spiritually minded and, therefore, least religious, are apt to be those who are brought up in luxury, protected by every possible form of human security, with no danger apparently to fear or enemies to contend with. It is not until the Master permits Satan to test them like Job with disease, the desertion of friends, the privation of property or character, that they begin to realize that there is a superior power, a ruling Providence. "When it thundered we believed Jove to reign,"[1] wrote the most famous of the Latin poets, who died only eight years before Jesus of Nazareth was born.

[1] Cœlo tonantem credidimus Jovem Regnare.

Who has ever lived long in the world without sharing the aspiration of the Royal Psalmist,

"Lead me, O Lord, to a Rock that is higher than I"?

VIII

Though the nature and terms of the problem under discussion imply, if it is not expressed, that it is to be determined by human reason alone, of course the most conclusive testimony as to the existence of life beyond the grave which is to be found in the Word, more commonly known as the Bible, because of its claim to a supernatural origin is excluded; but among the documents included in all modern editions of the Bible there are some letters which cannot be excluded on that ground, and which afford us about as unassailable testimony to the perpetuity of human life as can be found for any historic event recorded prior to the Christian era. Paul, a Jew of Tarsus, was a contemporary of Jesus of Nazareth, and but ten years his senior. When approaching

middle life. Paul was converted to an absolute faith in the mission of Jesus, of whose
doctrines and disciples he had theretofore
been the most conspicuous of persecutors.
He then became a missionary of the Christian faith to the Gentiles. Our Bible contains
several of his letters. In the Fifteenth Chapter
of his first letter to the Corinthians he says:

"Now I make known unto you, brethren, the
Gospel which I preached unto you, which also ye
received, wherein also ye stand, by which also ye
are saved. . . . Christ died for our sins, according
to the Scriptures, and that He was buried and that
He hath been raised on the third day, according to
the Scriptures, and that He appeared to Cephas,
then to the twelve, then he appeared to above five
hundred brethren at once, of whom the greater part
remain until now, but some are fallen asleep; then
He appeared to James, then to all the apostles,
and, last of all, as unto one born out of due time,
He appeared to me also, for I am the least of the
apostles that am not meet to be called an apostle
because I persecuted the Church of God."

This statement of the reappearance of
Jesus after His crucifixion is as authentic
evidence of a future life as any fact accred-

ited to Plato or to Aristotle or to Thucydides or even to Horace or Plutarch, for of none of these writers any more than of St. Paul have we any autograph manuscript; and yet the young men of all the universities of importance are still taught to study such of their writings as have survived them, and to give them the credit of doing their best to tell what at the time they believed and thought and taught. It is more difficult for a rational man to doubt that Paul believed that five hundred people saw Jesus after His resurrection, that the apostles or that he himself saw Him also after His resurrection and for a period, and that He was visible to some of them for more than a month, than it is to doubt that the life of Socrates was terminated by drinking hemlock, or that Plato and Xenophon are responsible authors for that story. All human testimony is liable to be fallible, but if any human testimony is credible, what is more credible than Paul's testimony of the appearance of Jesus to himself and to His disciples after His crucifixion, and what better proof of a future life can be asked or desired?

70

IX

But there is evidence of the perpetuity of life even more incontestable because many centuries more modern than Paul's, and proportionately more easy to be authenticated.

Emanuel Swedenborg—quite the most illustrious scientist of his generation; whose views not only of human life in this world but in the Great Beyond it is no longer fashionable to deride, and whose expositions of the interior or spiritual significance of the Word of God are talked of and accredited now to a constantly increasing extent, and proclaimed in pretty much every written language of every civilized country—in the fourth decade of his life became endowed with a gift of spiritual vision of the same kind as that which appears to have been vouchsafed to the Hebrew prophets, and especially to the inspired editor of the Apocalypse. He appears to have been directed by the Lord to explain with great fulness the interior or spiritual meaning of the Word of God, for which exposition the world had not been prepared at the time He was manifested in the flesh, nor even when the canon of our Bible was determined. In these his moments of super-sensuous life Swedenborg was permitted to visit the spiritual world where the enfranchised spirits from this terrestrial life are congregated. In the third volume of the *Arcana Cœlestia*, the most voluminous of his works, we find the following statement of an incident which occurred to its author while thus admitted to a personal intercourse with the world of disembodied spirits:

"Among the Gentiles, however, just as among Christians, there are both the wise and the simple. In order that I might be instructed as to the quality of these, it has been granted me to speak with both wise and simple, sometimes for hours and days. But of the wise there are scarcely any at this day [1750], whereas in ancient times there were many, especially in the Ancient Church, from which wisdom emanated to many nations. In order that I might know of what quality these were, I have been allowed to hold familiar converse with some of them, so that the nature of their wisdom and its superiority to that of the present day may be seen from what follows.

"There was present with me a certain person who was formerly among the *more wise,* and was thereby *well known in the learned world.* I conversed with him on various subjects, and as I knew that he had been a wise man, I spoke with him concerning wisdom, intelligence, order, the Word, and finally concerning the Lord. Concerning wisdom he said that there is no other wisdom than that which is of Life, and that wisdom can be predicted of nothing else. Concerning intelligence he said that it was from wisdom. Concerning order he said that it is from the Supreme God, and that to live in that order is to be wise and intelligent. As regards the Word, when I read to him something from the prophecies, he was very greatly delighted, especially from the fact that each of the names and each of the words signified interior things, wondering greatly that the learned of this day are not delighted with such a study. I plainly perceived that the interiors of his thought or mind had been opened, and at the same time that those of certain Christians who were present had been closed; for ill-will against him prevailed with them, and also unbelief that the Word is of this nature. Nay, when I went on reading the Word, he said that he could not be present, because he perceived it to be too holy for him to endure, so interiorly was he affected. The Christians, on the other hand, said aloud that they could be present; and this was because their interiors had been closed, and therefore the holy things did not affect them. At length I talked with him about the Lord; that He was born a man, but was conceived of God; that He had put off the human and had put on the divine; and that it is He who governs the universe. To this he made answer that he knew many things about the Lord, and perceived in his own way that it could not have been done otherwise if the human race was to be saved. Meantime certain wicked Christians injected various difficulties, for which he did not care, saying that it was not surprising, because they had become imbued in the life of the body with unbecoming ideas respecting these things, and that until such ideas were dispersed they could not admit things confirmatory, as could those who are ignorant. *This man was a Gentile.*"

In another of Swedenborg's works entitled *Cœlo et Inferno* (Heaven and Hell) —all his theological works were written in Latin—we find that the Gentile here referred to was Marcus Tullius Cicero, as appears by the following paragraph:

"322. There are among Gentiles, as among Christians, both wise and simple. That I might be instructed as to their quality, it has been given me to speak with both, sometimes for hours and days. But at this day there are no such wise ones as in ancient times, especially in the Ancient Church, which was spread through a large part of the Asiatic world, and from which religion emanated to many nations. That I might know their quality, it has been granted me to have familiar conversation with some of these wise men. There was a certain one with me who was among the wiser men of his time, and consequently well known in the learned world, with whom I conversed on various subjects: I was given to believe that it was Cicero.

75

And because I knew that he was a wise man, I conversed with him about wisdom, intelligence, order, and the Word."

Then follow almost a verbatim repetition of the words quoted above from the *Arcana Cœlestia*. It is a fact of incomparable interest and importance, when considered in connection with this spiritual interview, that Cicero, the reported Gentile, was in his temporal life a profound believer in the Unity of the Godhead, in the Divine origin of Life, and in the divine origin of all creative power; and that his standard of morals, as described in his writings, was as high, perhaps higher, than that of most professing Christians of even our own time. The evidences may be found in the imaginary "Dream of Scipio," recorded in his *Republica*, and in his *Tusculanes*, and in his *De Officiis*. The latter was a Latin text-book in the college in which I was educated.

I can imagine no one who shall have read with a mind open to the reception of truth for truth's sake, being able to doubt for one moment any one of the facts stated in these paragraphs by Swedenborg, or could believe that a man whose life was a model of every virtue, and whose reputation was even more spotless than that of any of the disciples of Jesus is reported to have been, could have deliberately not only reported, but have written down in two separate and independent works at different times, of course, precisely the same account of his conversation with an eminent Roman citizen who had died seventeen centuries at least before he was born.

I cannot help thinking this the most important evidence the world has outside of the Bible not only of a Future Life, but even of Cicero's authorship of the Works from which I have quoted as his.

I must now ask the indulgent reader's attention to extracts from Cicero's writings, which may serve to explain why Swedenborg found him seventeen centuries later among those Gentile Spirits noted for their wisdom.

In the sixty-second year of his age Cicero lost his lovely daughter Tullia, still in her childhood. His affliction was so great in consequence that he abandoned public life

77

and devoted himself to philosophical studies at one of his several country homes. At his Tusculan villa he spent five days in discussing with certain of his friends questions to which the bereavement may have given peculiar—may I not add Providential?—importance, such as:

How to contemn the terrors of death;

How to support affliction with fortitude;

How to submit to the accidents of life;

How to moderate our passions; and

How to explain the sufficiency of virtue to make us happy.

These five conferences he published under the title of Tusculan Disputations.

The following extracts are sufficient to reveal the rock foundation of Cicero's faith, both in the perpetuity of Life and the absolute Unity of the Godhead, of which Swedenborg is perhaps in many respects the most veridical of all witnesses.

"The greatest proof of all is, that Nature herself gives a silent judgment in favor of the immortality of the soul, inasmuch as all are anxious, and that to a great degree, about the things which concern futurity—

'One plants what future ages shall enjoy,'

as Statius saith in his Synephebi. What is his object in doing so, except that he is interested in posterity? Shall the industrious husbandman, then, plant trees the fruit of which he shall never see? And shall not the great man found laws, institutions, and a republic? What does the procreation of children imply—and our care to continue our names—and our adoptions—and our scrupulous exactness in drawing up wills—and the inscriptions on monuments, and panegyrics, but that our thoughts run on futurity? There is no doubt but a judgment may be formed of nature in general, from looking at each nature in its most perfect specimens; and what is a more perfect specimen of a man than those who look on themselves as born for the assistance, the protection, and the preservation of others?" . . .

"Hercules has gone to heaven; he would never have gone thither had he not whilst amongst men prepared the way himself. These are all of ancient dates, and have besides the sanction of universal religions.[1]

"For, if those men now think that they have attained something who have seen the mouth of the Pontus, and those straits which were passed by the ship called *Argo*, because,

From Argos she did chosen men convey,
Bound to fetch back the golden fleece, their prey;

or those who have seen the straits of the ocean,

Where the swift waves divide the neighbouring
  shores
Of Europe, and of Afric,

[1] This paragraph may have suggested to the most illustrious historian of the Imperial Annals of Rome his notable hypothesis, "*Si quis piorum monitus locus,*" etc., so happily parodied by the most eminent poet of the Victorian era in the following lines:

"Yet if, as holiest men have deem'd, there be
  A land of souls beyond that sable shore
To shame the doctrine of the Sadducee
  And sophist, madly vain of dubious lore,
How sweet it were in concert to adore
  With those who made our mortal labours light,
To hear each voice we fear'd to hear no more,
  Behold each mighty shade reveal'd to sight,
The Bactrian, Samian sage, and all who taught the right."
                                    —*Childe Harold*, ii, 8.

what kind of sight do you imagine that will be, when the whole earth is laid open to our view? and that, too, not only in its position, form, and boundaries, nor those parts of it only which are habitable, but those also that lie uncultivated, through the extremities of heat and cold to which they are exposed; for not even now is it with our eyes that we view what we see, for the body itself has no senses; but (as the naturalists, aye, and even the physicians assure us, who have opened our bodies, and examined them), there are certain perforated channels from the seat of the soul to the eyes, ears, and nose; so that frequently, when either prevented by meditation, or the force of some bodily disorder, we neither hear nor see, though our eyes and ears are open, and in good condition; so that we may easily apprehend that it is the soul itself which sees and hears, and not those parts which are, as it were, but windows to the soul; by means of which, however, it can perceive nothing, unless it is on the spot, and exerts itself. How shall we account for the fact that by the same power of thinking we comprehend the most different things,

as color, taste, heat, smell, and sound?
which the Soul could never know by her five
messengers, unless everything was referred
to her, and she were the sole judge of all.
And we shall certainly discover these things
in a more clear and perfect degree when the
soul is disengaged from the body, and has
arrived at that goal to which nature leads
her; for at present, notwithstanding nature
has contrived, with the greatest skill, those
channels which lead from the body to the
soul, yet are they, in some way or other,
stopped up with earthy and concrete bodies;
but when we shall be nothing but soul, then
nothing will interfere to prevent our seeing
everything in its real substance, and in its
true character. . . .

"But there are many who press the opposite side of this question, and condemn
souls to death, as if they were criminals
capitally convicted; nor have they any other
reason to allege why the immortality of the
soul appears to them to be incredible, except
that they are not able to conceive what sort
of thing the soul can be when disentangled
from the body; just as if they could really

form a correct idea as to what sort of thing it is, even when it is in the body; what its form, and size, and abode are; so that were they able to have a full view of all that is now hidden from them in a living body, they have no idea whether the soul would be discernable by them, or whether it is of so fine a texture that it would escape their sight. Let those consider this, who say that they are unable to form any idea of the soul without the body, and then they will see whether they can form any adequate idea of what it is when it is in the body. For my own part, when I reflect on the nature of the soul, it appears to me a far more perplexing and obscure question to determine what is its character while it is in the body—a place which, as it were, does not belong to it—than to imagine what it is when it leaves it, and has arrived at the free æther, which is, if I may so say, its proper, its own habitation. For unless we are to say that we cannot apprehend the character or nature of anything which we have never seen, we certainly may be able to form some notion of God, and of the divine soul when released from the body.

Dicæarchus, indeed, and Aristoxenus, because it was hard to understand the existence, and substance, and nature of the soul, asserted that there was no such thing as a soul at all. It is, indeed, the most difficult thing imaginable, to discern the soul by the soul. And this, doubtless, is the meaning of the precept of Apollo, which advises every one to *Know Himself*. For I do not apprehend the meaning of the god to have been, that we should understand our members, our stature, and form; for we are not merely bodies; nor, when I say these things to you, am I addressing myself to your body: when, therefore, he says, 'Know Yourself,' he says this, 'Inform yourself of the nature of your soul'; for the body is but a kind of vessel, or receptacle of the soul, and whatever your soul does is your own act. To know the soul, then, unless it had been divine, would not have been a precept of such excellent wisdom, as to be attributed to a god; but even though the soul should not know of what nature itself is, will you say that it does not even perceive that it exists at all, or that it has motion? on which is founded that reason of Plato's, which is explained by Socrates in the Phædrus, and inserted by me, in my sixth book of the Republic:

"'That which is always moved is eternal; but that which gives motion to something else, and is moved itself by some external cause, when that motion ceases, must necessarily cease to exist. That, therefore, alone which is self-moved, because it is never forsaken by itself, can never cease to be moved. Besides, it is the beginning and principle of motion to everything else; but whatever is a principle has no beginning, for all things arise from that principle, and it cannot itself owe its use to anything else; for then it would not be a principle did it proceed from anything else. But if it has no beginning, it never will have any end; for a principle which is once extinguished, cannot itself be restored by anything else, nor can it produce anything else from itself; inasmuch as all things must necessarily arise from some first cause. And thus it comes about, that the first principle of motion must arise from that thing which is itself moved by itself; and that can neither have a beginning nor an end of its existence, for otherwise the whole heaven and earth would be overset, and all nature would stand still, and not be able to acquire any force, by the impulse of which it might be first set in motion. Seeing, then, that it is clear, that whatever moves itself is eternal, can there be any doubt that the soul is so? For everything is inanimate which is moved by an external force, which also belongs to itself. For this is the peculiar nature and power of the soul; and if the soul be the only thing in the whole world which has the power of self-motion, then certainly it never had a beginning, and therefore it is eternal.'"

There are many, perhaps a majority, who do not trouble themselves much with speculations about the probability or improbability of a future life. Most people in their youth and early manhood are apt to be so much interested in the present that they can hardly be called believers or deniers of a future life; but I think it rarely if ever happens that any person *takes up arms against the doctrine of a future life from any lack of testimony,* or, indeed, for any other reason than a more or less morbid attachment to what he regards as the pleasures of the present one. Was it not that pathetic conviction to which Jesus gave utterance in His pictorial way when a certain man said unto Him, "I will follow Thee whithersoever Thou goest"?

"The foxes have holes, and the birds of the air have nests, but the Son of Man hath not where to lay His head." Not even in the breast of the disciple who promised so bravely.

From a photograph, copyright, 1902, by J. E. Purdy, Boston

JULIA   WARD   HOWE

Beyond the Veil

Julia Ward Howe

IV

𝔅𝔢𝔶𝔬𝔫𝔡 𝔱𝔥𝔢 𝔙𝔢𝔦𝔩

I AM invited to write a paper of some two thousand words on the subject of Immortality. I accept this invitation to discourse in print upon a theme which has long been familiar to me. I believe that some part of me is immortal. I have always so believed. It should be easy to give some account of the why and wherefore of this belief, yet, strange to say, I do not find it so. The effort of many days has only produced a certain set of disjointed statements which, although in no wise contradictory to one another, cannot, with my poor skill, be made to introduce and explain one another. Perhaps the best thing I can attempt will be to examine briefly what I really think about a future life, and, if possible, why I think so and not otherwise.

To begin, then, with the simple notions of my childhood. I was born in a world in which the belief in a future life was almost unquestioned. The blessedness of heaven and the torment of hell were presented to my infant imagination as the ultimates of my good or ill conduct in every-day life. Like most other children, I believed what I was told, and in general tried to obey the commands of my elders. I loved to hear about the heavenly life, which somehow seemed to furnish the skyscape of my days as they were added in weeks, months, and years. I recall having once made an offering to the God of my childish prayers. The altar was a little stool, the sacrifice some small objects which I supposed to be of value. I remember also refusing to say my prayers to a new nursery assistant, because it did not appear to me fitting to take a stranger into my confidence, a scruple which the authorities of the same nursery speedily overruled.

Wordsworth has said:

"Heaven lies about us in our infancy,
    And trailing clouds of glory do we come
    From God, who is our home."

And later, Emerson says of Michel Angelo,

"Himself from God he could not free."

Even so naturally did my idea of merit include a divine Absolute, whom to please or displease would furnish the tests of good or ill conduct.

Let us pass over many years of experience, individual, mostly not unusual, and come to where the enlightened intellect of the twentieth century finds itself obliged to stand. It is perforce an age of question, and all thought which penetrates below the surface of things must take this attitude of interrogation, which should be reverent, and which may be insolent. In the first place, this wonder book, the Bible. Is it an exception to all human rules and laws of action? Did the ancient chroniclers do their best to set down the record of Creation and its consequences? Did the psalmist, the prophet, the moralist, each in turn contribute his highest human power of expression and forethought to this marvellous treasure of an Eastern people? Or did the living God of Israel dictate the volume, chapter, and verse to scribes especially selected? Once this question would have been held to be impious. Now it is inevitable; and if the Book is a human work its contents must be judged by human standards.

Supposing this to be so decided, the systems of promise and of threat which men have built upon it are also without the authority of the absolute, and our dreams of an endless future of recompense, painful or pleasurable, for the deeds done in the body, have all the qualities of dreams and none other.

What then? Have we lost our God? Never for one moment. Unspeakable, He is, the beneficent parent, the terrible, incorruptible judge, the champion of the innocent, the accuser of the guilty, refuge, hope, redeemer, friend; neither palace walls nor prison cells can keep Him out. Every step of our way from the birth hour He has gone with us. Were we at the gallows' foot, and deservedly, He would leave a sweet drop in the cup of death. He would measure suffering to us, but would forbid despair. The victory of goodness must be complete.

The lost sheep must be found—ay, and the lost soul must turn to the way in which the peace of God prevails. We learn the dreadful danger of those who wander from the right path, but we may also learn the redeeming power which recalls and reclaims them.

So fade our heavens and hells. Christ, if He knew their secrets, did not betray them. On the boundless sea of conjecture we are still afloat, with such mental tools as we possess to guide us, with the skies, the stars, the seasons, seeking a harbor from which no voyager has ever returned.

So much, the later schemes of thought have taken from us. Shall we ask what they have given us in exchange for what we have lost?

It seems a little strange that with the accumulated wisdom and power of the ages a farmer's son of Massachusetts should have been the first clearly to enunciate this important phrase, "The transient and permanent in religion." We must have known of this distinction all along. In all that we think, and in much that we believe, constant growth and metamorphosis take pleace. Paul

says, "When I was a child, I thought as a
child; I believed as a child." How full of
beauty were these visions of childhood, but
also how evanescent, each evolving itself
into one more advanced in thought, in understanding, until the moment in which Love

"Smote the chord of self, that trembling
Passed in music out of sight."

Does our acquaintance with this wonder
world terminate with the days and years of
our age? Shall death forever divide us from
all the marvellous story of our spiritual experiences of evil seeming for a time to pre-
vail, of the blessed eternal good whose con-
quest of evil is certain and final?

Tell us, you stars mysteriously hung to
measure the depths of the heavens. Tell us,
thou pitiable, shameful way of excess and
error, with thy heroic redemption. Let the
Jew speak:

"Whither shall I go from Thy presence?
If I ascend into heaven, Thou art there. If
I make my bed in hell, behold! Thou art
there also."

Let the apostle speak: "Who shall sep-

96

arate us from the love of Christ?" In all these things we are conquerors, through Him that loved us, and loving once, loves ever.

To me has been granted a somewhat unusual experience of life. Ninety full years have been measured off to me, their lessons and opportunities unabridged by wasting disease or gnawing poverty. I have enjoyed general good health, comfortable circumstances, excellent company, and the incitements to personal effort which civilized society offers to its members. For this life and its gifts I am, I hope, devoutly thankful. I came into this world a helpless and ignorant bit of humanity. I have found in it many helps toward the attainment of my full human stature, material, mental, moral. In this slow process of attainment many features have proved transient. Visions have come and gone. Seasons have bloomed and closed, passions have flamed and faded. *Something* has never left me. My relation to it has suffered many changes, but it still remains, the foundation of my life, light in darkness, consolation in ill-fortune, guide in uncertainty.

In the nature of things, I must soon lose sight of this sense of constant metamorphosis whose limits bound our human life. How about this unchanging element? Will it die when I shall be laid in earth? The visible world has no answer to this question. For it, dead is dead, and gone is gone. But a deep spring of life within me says: "Look beyond. Thy days numbered hitherto register a divine promise. Thy mortal dissolution leaves this promise unfulfilled, but not abrogated. Thou mayst hope that all that made thy life divine will live for thine immortal part."

I have quoted Theodore Parker's great word, and have made no attempt, so far, to bring into view considerations which may set before us the fundamental distinction between what in human experience passes and what abides.

In the first place, human life passes, like other life. The splendid blossom, the noble fruit. Inquire into its power and glory after two-thirds of a century have passed over it. You will find weakness in the place of strength, the mournful attar of memory replacing as it can the fresh fragrance of hope. The bowed form suggests the segment of a mystic circle. The restricted mind turns its tools into toys. "They did not measure the infinite for us. Let us get from their uses such pleasure as we can."

Life passes, but the conditions of life do not. Air, food, water, the moral sense, the mathematical problem and its solution. These things wait upon one generation much as they did upon its predecessor. What, too, is this wonderful residuum which refuses to disappear when the very features of time seem to succumb to the law of change, and we recognize our world no more? Whence comes this system in which man walks as in an artificial frame, every weight and lever of which must correspond with the outlines of an eternal pattern?

Our spiritual life appears to include three terms in one. They are ever with us, this Past which does not pass, this Future which never arrives. They are part and parcel of this conscious existence which we call Present. While Past and Future have each their seasons of predominance, both are contained in the moment which is gone while we say, "It is here."

So the Eternal is with us, whether we will or not, and the idea of God is inseparable from the persuasion of immortality; the Being which, perfect in itself, can neither grow nor decline, nor indeed undergo any change whatever. The great Static of the universe, the rationale of the steadfast faith of believing souls, the sense of beauty which justifies our high enjoyments, the sense of proportion which upholds all that we can think about ourselves and our world, the sense of permanence which makes the child in very truth parent to the man, able to solve the deepest riddle, the profoundest problem in all that is. Let us then willingly take the Eternal with us in our flight among the suns and stars.

Experience is our great teacher, and on this point it is wholly wanting. No one on the farther side of the great Divide has been able to inform those on the hither side of what lies beyond.

Yet our whole life, rightly interpreted, shows us the never-failing mercy of a divine

Parent. We may ask, "Whither shall I go from Thy presence?" And we may answer, "Surely, goodness and mercy shall follow me all the days of my eternal life, and I shall dwell in the house of the Lord forever."

The anticipation of a life beyond the grave so belongs to our human mastery over the conditions of animal life that it seems to be an integral part of our human endowment.

We feel something in us that cannot die when blood and brain, muscle and tissue, have reached the brief and uncertain term of their service. For so long, the body can perform its functions and hold together, but what term is set for the soul? Nothing in its make-up foretokens a limited existence. Its sentence would seem to be, "Once and always."

The promise of a future life is held to have such prominence in Christ's teaching as to lead Paul to say that the Master "brought life and immortality to light." How did He do this? By filling the life of to-day with the consciousness of eternal things, of truths and principles which would not change if the whole visible universe were to pass away.

No one to-day, I think, will maintain that

Christ created the hope which He aroused to an activity before undreamed of. The majority of the Jews believed in a life after death, as is shown by the segregation of the Sadducees from the orthodox of the synagogue. The new teaching vindicated the spiritual rights and interests of man. From the depths of his own heart was evolved the consciousness of a good that could not die. Man, the creature of a day, has a vested interest in things eternal. The solid principles upon which the social world is organized, the laws of which Sophocles makes Antigone say that "they are not of to-day nor yesterday."

Creatures of a day as we seem, there is that in us which is older than the primeval rocks, than the υλη out of which this earth, our temporary dwelling-place, was made. The reason which placed the stars, the sense of proportion which we recognize in the planetary system, finds its correspondence in this brain of ours. We question every feature of what we see, think, and feel. We try every link of the chain and find it sound if we ourselves are sound. This power of remotest question and assent is not of to-day nor yesterday.

It transcends all bounds of time and space. It weighs the sun, explores the pathway of the stars, and writes, having first carefully read, the history of earth and heaven. It moves in company with the immortals. How much of it is mortal? Only so much as a small strip of earth can cover. These remains are laid away with reverence, having served their time. What has become of the wonderful power which made them alive? It belongs to that in nature which cannot die.

A babe wept on the borders of the Nile, a foundling, destined for death, but fated to dictate rules of action to the human world. How did this come about? The babe, rescued and grown to manhood, has come upon something as unchangeable as the law of numbers.

Oh, baby in the Nile shallows, wiser than the Sphinx; oh, saint in the Athenian prison; oh, discoverer of the second birth, regenerator of mankind—what do you teach us? The eternal hope which lies in God's eternal goodness. What is best for thee and me will be.

HENRY MILLS ALDEN

The Other Side of Mortality

Henry Mills Alden

V

𝔗𝔥𝔢 𝔒𝔱𝔥𝔢𝔯 𝔖𝔦𝔡𝔢 𝔬𝔣 𝔐𝔬𝔯𝔱𝔞𝔩𝔦𝔱𝔶

I

WHEN Tom Appleton, whose wit added much to the gayety of Boston and Newport fifty years ago, was told that he was about to die, he said, "How interesting!"

And really there is nothing so interesting as this dying. Not merely to those immediately confronting the great fascination, and many of these have not the wit to see it as that, or to regard it with the degree or kind of imaginative expectancy which the occasion warrants. The loving, who are left behind, may be excused for not looking upon the event in that light at all. The sense of loss blurs their vision, and when grief is assuaged by time the "world beyond" seems interesting chiefly because so many dear ones have passed thither.

Putting away the poignancy of separation from our thought of death, and thus becoming disinterested as to any purely personal point of view, we are possessed by a larger interest in mortality itself.

II

From its beginning, mortality has been bound up with love. There is no mortality in the inorganic world, none in the lowest order of organisms—the unicellular, in which there is propagation by simple fissure, the continuity never broken. The amœba of to-day is the original amœba. The one half of the cell, thus divided, was indistinguishable from the other. They were not mates—each *was* the other. How could the organic world escape this utterly unromantic identity?

If the cells could have held counsel together (and who knows what "holding counsel together," in ways unknown to us, there may have been) they would have agreed that such existence as they had was intolerable, each member of the whole assembly isolated and independent, none wanting anything of another. They would have had as wild desire for some kind of otherness as if they had been reading Prof. William James's *A Pluralistic Universe*. This desire was met by the specialization of sex, and with that came death, as if it were part and parcel of the great romance.

All that we can think of as interesting in organic existence followed—all the flora and fauna of this world. But every member of this higher order of beings must die; and each individual was made up of organs so mutually interdependent that the chances of death were multiplied.

We cannot look upon this mortality—thus associated with all the beauty and glory of the earth—as a penalty. It would seem rather to have been supremely desirable. Humanity, which would have been impossible but for this higher and more complex organization—in which partition is for the sake of union—shares most largely and deeply in its beauty, glory, and romance. Why is it, then, that man alone should protest against the complementary term and look upon death—just because of its intimate and inevitable association with love and whatever is lovely—as the supreme irony? However we may account for it—most reasonably, perhaps, because man alone has developed a tragic sense which inclines him to magnify the pathos of his own story—it is certainly not a normal or natural view, not an acceptance of life upon its own terms.

Besides, it is a most ungracious attitude. Mortality is chiefly interesting because it belongs to the Kingdom of Grace. The association of it with the Realm of Law—or, rather, the kind of conception of that association which has generally been entertained —has been the gravest of human mistakes. It is true that we comprehend the law only when we see it as love. But men have not thus comprehended it, and this failure has been most apparent in the kind of connection which they have insisted upon between death and law—as if Nature were punitive and death the abhorred penalty she holds over us, inevitable finally in any case, but also forever impending. All the perverted conceptions that have been entertained of God and Nature began with this false idea of death as something terrible—this death which had come into the world before there was anything that could be thought of as punishable or as in any way other than it should be, and which, ever since it began to be, had been bound up with natural law as it had been with love in an association as beautiful as it is possible for us to imagine.

But the more we look upon the world as a continuous creation—a constant becoming —the grace of it all impresses us rather than the law of it, which, after all, is only our mental generalization. Harmony is inherent in creation, where everything is fit in becoming at all. This identity of "becomingness" with "fitness" is registered in our common speech. "Grace" is a more expressive word than "fitness," because it is more intimate to the thought of creative and abounding life. The very fact, then, that mortality is, that it became—in the series of becomings— that it is inevitable in the higher order of organic existence, that it is inseparable from every quality which makes them beautiful or interesting, should not only quell in us any doubts or fears concerning it, but convince us of its grace and bounty.

The more we ourselves are in the Kingdom of Grace—the more we are Christians, following the Master's own thought and leading—the more gracious and significant will this mortality seem to us. They who live sordid lives, full of greed, envy, and ambition, are hostile to death, which loosens their tenacious grasp of earthly prizes. There is in our loves a nobler kind of avarice which denies to death the full measure of its sweetness and worth. But the first word or token of the spiritual life is Release—we lose to find. We give up, without the thought of gain for ourselves, just for the sake of others, even "in honor preferring one another." We do not thus yield because we ought; it is a vital and spontaneous altruism. It is by a natural grace—I had almost said politeness —that one generation gives place to another, and the courtesy is more appreciable because it is not sudden, but waits to yield a maturity of service in a gradual and deliberately conscious descension. This grace of waiting leads to the development of all the domestic

112

and social graces—the amenities and sympathies which are the heart culture of humanity. This culture could never, in any generation, have been so quick and zestful save in the face of death, and it could not have attained its present scope and variety, forever retaining its freshness, but for its constant renewal and increase with each successive generation. And if we consider the culture of the mind and soul, beyond the range of the affections, prompted by disinterested curiosity, as summed up in human science, art, and imaginative literature, we see that it could never have had a beginning, any initial impulse, in a race whose continuance upon the earth was stable, not broken by mortality and renewed by nativity. What stimulus to growth, what possibilities of expansion, would Imagination have in that level and sterile world?

III

Divest man of his mortality, then all that remains to him as an investment loses its value. As a denizen of the earth, he would be placed in a situation involving the dullest irony, supposing that on such terms he could have life at all, or partnership with the living world about him—really an untenable hypothesis, since there is no life we know the other side of which (and that side next and most intimate) is not death, no participation in any life without partaking also of mortality. But granted the anomaly, there is the irony. Every living thing else is part of an ever-changing scene, budding, blossoming, fruit-bearing, decaying. The seasons come and go. The meanest seed may die and from its grave have quick ascent and increase. He alone dryly abides; for him no passing, no increment. This is an irony by the side of which that poignant irony which pierces his heart because all that is loveliest must die and he too must die, leaving behind all that he most loves, is surpassingly interesting; and indeed he makes the most of its pathos and romance in his art and in his literature.

The romance of death, while it is so large an element in our appreciation of it, is never quite dissociated from its pathos.

The mere body of death has no attraction for us; we instinctively put it away from us and bury it out of sight. Death itself repudiates it and refuses to be defined in terms of a corruption which no longer lies next to such life as it has served but which belongs to purely physical forces outside of its kingdom. What life has abandoned death also has left behind.

As I have said, life has no romance save in the face of death. While we live, the physiological reaction is measured by the extent and quickness of our dying. Sleep, which is at once our undoing and our recreation, would abortively fall short of its full meaning were it not the image of death; and the dream in like manner lose its subtle complement. The psychical reaction is of greater moment. The term of life is marked by a limited cycle, enclosing for each of us our individual experience. At every point of advance there is a new horizon. When we reach the end—what then? There could be no greater challenge to the imagination. This is the largest romance death offers. But within the cycle there is at every step the thanatopsis. History is the record not only of past times, but of a humanity that *has* passed—an unreturning host, of whom but few in any generation have left so much as their names behind them. But for this passing and the human sense of it there would have been no record at all, and no motive for preservative art. *Sic transit:* and because glory was of the transient deed, and beauty of forms that vanish, there was the quick sense of these and the desire to hold them in arrest, as the poet and the sculptor hold them.

Death has always haunted the poet's thought, insisting upon its own note, piercing or pensive, in every imaginative creation—against it in bold relief must stand heroism, love, and friendship. In tragedy it was death out of time or precipitated by mysterious fate that heightened the pathetic moment as in the epic it had heightened the heroic. Iphigenia, whose story would seem to intimate that there was in the untimely death of the victim something so sharply sweet to the gods that it turned them from wrath to mercy, was for Euripides what Patroclus was for Homer.

The grief in Shelley's *Adonais*, in Milton's *Lycidas*, and in Tennyson's *In Memoriam* is set against death, thus untimely, in gentler relief.

Very different from the pathos, mingled with our æsthetic impressions, which we feel in this distant contemplation of death face to face with a life indirectly presented to us in art or literature and in every chapter of human history, is that which we feel in our immediate experience. The poet may express the thought and sentiment of it for us in pertinent phrase and illuminating metaphor, but not the reality of it; nor can I attempt to express that for my readers.

IV

This pathos is too deep for tears, and the sombre habiliments of mourning contradict rather than express its true meaning. Blackness befits the dulness of despair, not the quickness of this grief for loved ones lost. If the angel of death is not here the angel of life, then indeed has his brightness vanished and we are duped by mortality. No!

Here more than anywhere death is the quickener of human hearts, expanding hope, faith, and love beyond all visible limitations. The curtain folding us closely about unfolds to another light, as night unveils the stars. The sharpest grief pierces into this strange brightness.

Our praise of mortality therefore halts not because of the keen affliction that has first pierced our hearts, but—to use Isaiah's phrase—with "a sword bathed in heaven." Herein, indeed, lies the chief value of mortality,—that, closing one door, it opens another, never leaving life's thoroughfare for the byways of corruption. "Let the dead bury its dead." Death speaks in the words of the Master, "Come thou and follow me." It is not yet our own time to follow, but we hear the voice, and we see in swift vision the winged Psyche free of her chrysalis.

v

Life takes the highway, which never even skirts the tomb. It is the highway of endless change. It was the way of the physical world before death entered it—that world which seems to us uniform and immutable because its transformations have so vast a scale and scope that the latest of them was earlier than anything we call living. Beyond that, the retrospect is hidden from us. Possibly it was from the beginning a living universe. But now, in our strange partnership with it, we are sensible only of the side turned to us—its dying side—its descent for our rising, and in our fancy we picture to ourselves its long course of decadence before its gracious abeisance to the Cell. Of its ascending side we know nothing. Perhaps mutation is a truer word for its procession than evolution. Certainly it is a truer word for the procession of what we call life—truest of all for the human soul on its pathway here and hereafter, with Death for its shining leader, whose torch is never inverted. The light of this torch, while it is thrown forward farther than our eyes can see, is also forever turned backward upon our earthly life, by its illumination revealing the glory of that life more and more, from generation to generation; and the light is more and more the light of love, since Death is forever bound up with Love.

Hence the growth of a deeper humanism from age to age, through changes in emotional and psychical sensibility — changes which cannot be accounted for by natural selection and which involve surprises not precalculable. New interests and new motives emerge, new beauty, new truth, and a new sense of life. The changes are more rapid with every generation because we oppose less resistance to the current whose pulsations are death, in the falling, and birth in the rising—the systole and diastole. We more willingly let old things pass into new, while we pass with them, yielding to the stream without misgiving. This it is to have faith in life through comprehension of death.

VI

Looking beyond the term of individual life, we are thus better prepared to expect a new surprise, of which we seem to catch a radiant glimpse. It cannot be otherwise than that a marvellous change awaits us, though we know not what it is.

Some of us who are nearing or have passed the scripturally allotted term have been asked to say in this collection of essays what we think and feel concerning this matter. We may well be supposed to find the theme more interesting—the romance of it more inviting. For us the land slopes down, with a western exposure, to the Garden of Hesperides whose apples are golden, and we breathe fragrant airs from an unknown sea suggesting the new adventure. But that sea is hidden from us, as from all others, until we fall asleep.

Our mature experience avails not, except by way of preparation if we have acquired the habit of dying, thus making the most of the life that now is for all of its values — by the closest culture of its whole field.

Our experience does not enable us to know ourselves—that larger part of us which creatively determines the scope of our powers, the mutations of our sensibility, and the very physiognomy of individual bodies and souls. All this is hidden from us, though it is the ground of our experience in this earthly life. The ground of our mystical partnership with Nature is also hidden, as is the bond of our kinship with all life; yet these are natively our heritage. We have, as natively, a real knowledge of this continuity as something implicit and unbroken.

But what we know *about* ourselves or the world outside of us is only that which is definable in our consciousness through discontinuity and disintegration, so that we express judgments or discriminations. To define is to note the limit, the line of cleavage, the contour. We call the words by which we do this "terms," as denoting endings. We know in this explicit way only the boundaries of things and, of things that pass, the interruption of the current. We bind like things together by a mental process of classification, which is not reintegration, and arrive at general concepts. Thus we have *formal* as distinguished from *real* knowledge, because we have "discourse of reason," because we have intellects which react upon the phenomena of the world and of our experience, defining them, making inductive and deductive judgments concerning them, reducing them to systems in our minds—all of which we express in our speech. It is a very important kind of knowledge, such as pertains distinctively to human intelligence. It has the same relation to the development of human thought that experimentation has to material and social progress, but a very much larger range. We think about everything, and our speculation seems to gain greater facility when it passes beyond all the data of our observation and experience. Our abstract conceptions, especially when we can express them in words beginning with a capital letter, like "Absolute" and "Infinite," have a kind of tyranny over us. Our philosophical speculation from Plato to our own time, as Professor James has shown in his latest book, is made up mostly of these imposing but empty abstractions.

This "thin" philosophy, as Professor James expressively calls it, cannot help us to any real sense of our present existence and still less of the life to come. Our thought about a future life, however "thin," when it takes the shape of a theory, has some "thickness" from the desire for the continuity in that life of the individual consciousness and for conscious reunion with loved ones who have gone before. It would seem strange to us that, in connection with the resurrections recorded in the Gospel, no light should have been thrown upon these points—that, indeed, no questions concerning them seem to have been put to the risen Lazarus by his friends or to the risen Christ by His disciples. But we must remember that then, as during the whole time then past since the beginning of history, there was no margin for curiosity about these things, since everybody knew all about them. There were no questions to be put. Not only was there no doubt, there was absolutely fixed certitude. The geography of the underworld was more accurately known than that of the next province on the earth's surface.

The question, "If a man die, shall he live again?" is as old as philosophy itself—but it was not a question with the common, unspeculative people of the ancient world. Now everybody thinks, and where there is no doubt as to the main issue there is frequently solicitude as to this one point—the survival of individual consciousness, the interest in which is heightened by, and for many quite dependent upon, the possibility of future reunions of families and friends with full mutual recognition.

VII

As to this concern regarding the future restoration of intimacies broken by death, a careful study of the record of any community would show how much more stress very many people put upon it as related to the future than as related to the present life—which does not seem quite consistent. Homes are broken otherwise than by death—forever, in the most natural way, by the marriages of the younger generation for the making of new homes. Separations and divorces break the most intimate of human ties, and those who are widowed in many instances marry again. An adopted child often

125

displaces one that has been early lost and, after years of cherishment, would not be given up even for the one that is gone. We do not love because the object is lovable; the object is lovable because we can love. Then, too, we reflect that, though we may have lived before this life, we do not seem to miss anything from past lives; on the contrary, we would stoutly aver that those we most dearly love we have always loved in however many lives have been ours. Still, so strong is the sentiment by which we would cling to our dear ones for all lives to come, even though we call it the avarice of love, that it is painful to discuss it as if it were a question. The sentiment will persist to the end of human time; and as love grows more and more in the world, excluding hate, and is more luminous and significant, being constantly lifted to a higher plane of finer feeling, so that what is elemental and instinctive in natural ties not only shows leaf and flower rather than root, but takes on psychical veils, it seems more intelligently to demand expansion beyond the limits of the present earthly life.

126

VIII

And it is just this demand for expansion, for fuller development, which prompts the desire for a continuation hereafter of our identical individuality, even if there could be no renewal of earthly associations. Those who have the largest development here have the keenest expectation of the future and would be satisfied with the assurance of just enough reminiscence of this life to establish the sense of continuity. More than that might be distressfully confusing, involving a sacrifice of all the advantages of individuality itself. I would rather give up the reminiscence altogether than these very appreciable advantages. The Occidental mind does not take kindly to the conception of Nirvana. Nothing could be "thinner" than that. We would rather wait for a new universe—and the wait would not be sensibly as long as that between going to sleep and waking— and have back some sort of bodies, with a comfortable sequestration of our individual souls, and all the beautiful and varied cosmic phenomena about us to which we have been accustomed, than to be suddenly and forever swallowed up in the inane Absolute. If we care so much for recognizable identity we should doubtless, in the new-born universe, have sometimes that sense of familiarity, seeming like a reminiscence, which we are now often surprised into by some especially novel scene or situation. We might really be very much like our old selves and the world about us substantially the same as this, for our study and delight. The Demiurge, it is true, may be Protean, beyond our possible imagining, and the whole investment might be a surprising transformation, even bafflingly unanological to anything we know. We might have transformed capacities and faculties and not miss old things or any reminders of them. Of course, then as now, we might regard the whole thing as illogical and see how it might have been better fashioned, but it would be new. We may reasonably suppose, if our reasoning counts for anything, that each new universe, if not better than its predecessor, would be an advance. There may be a comparative modernity in universes.

But I am not propounding this as even

a working hypothesis of a future life. For all we know, instead of universes proceeding *in tandem*, a new universe is now rising synchronously with the falling of this one, involving as this evolves—as the new year of a tree begins with its exfoliation. We see only the katabolism, the expenditure, the descent. The tension side is hidden from us. But, as to any application to our theme, that also is a theory. I am casting about for any, even plausible, chance of being saved from absorption into the Absolute.

IX

What I would fain insist upon is individuality. Continued individuality from one life to another seems to involve a contradiction of terms. Formed life—that structural result of habit which we call character, our developed tastes, and our intellectual attainments—we can hardly conceive of as carried over into a future existence whose emergence is even newer than birth. But most people do so conceive, however unphilosophical the conception may be; they think of that other life as beginning just where it stops here and going right on from that point. Evidently the Society for Psychical Research rests its whole procedure upon this assumption, and if the expectations of most of the members of this society should be satisfactorily realized in verifiable proofs of this hypothesis, what can the candid philosopher do but accept it? On the other hand, we cannot positively assert that because it is not proven it is therefore untenable. We do not, perhaps, comprehend to what extent our mental fabric is undone in sleep and rises again, renewed by the re-creative office of this same sleep. Is there in death some like miracle of release and restoration, the soul receiving back its proper vesture, wholly fresh and mystically transformed by the very power that wrought the ruinous divestiture? We do not know—but if it is so, is it necessary or of any value to the soul that its reinvestment should include the complete equipment it acquired on earth—of information, technical skill, and practical maxims, along with the trivial curiosity of a gossip? Is there no absolution in the great change? Must we think of these souls as forever waiting, as we imagine the Martians to be, for the chance of a casual communication with us?

The conservation of individuality would, with this handicap, seem less desirable. We would have it as light-weighted, at least, as we have it here and now. We value it in the present life for its inviolate insulation, which at the same time shuts us in from distracting interruptions and leaves us open to the larger invisible currents of life. It is the essential of perfect accord with other souls. Thus, while it seems a kind of discontinuity by reason of its sequestration, individuality serves the continuity of life. But it does not make that continuity, which is indeed the first premise of all existence.

We think ourselves as being here and now; it is the way of our thinking—the only way in which we can think at all. By the same formal habit of the mind we think of dying as going elsewhere, and speak of being "launched from time into eternity." But this phraseology is not applicable to the spirit itself. Distance is not real, but an illusion. The earth never *really* left the sun. Because of its apparent separation, which emphasizes the bond of union, it becomes the explicit expression of solarity. Eternity is not quantitative; it is the quality of this life as truly as it can be of any other. Resurgence is an essential attribute of life; it is not a coming or a going, but a new becoming.

X

As mortality was not always, so it may not always be. Before it, was a lower order of life—beyond it, may be some higher order. So said the Master—that in the world to come there is no marrying or giving in marriage; neither shall they die any more. Sex and mortality began together and together they cease. The life without these and beyond these, as we know them, transcends our comprehension.

We confront the great change not with a theory, but as our most interesting venture.

THOMAS   WENTWORTH   HIGGINSON

The Future Life

Thomas Wentworth Higginson

VI

𝔗𝔥𝔢 𝔉𝔲𝔱𝔲𝔯𝔢 𝔏𝔦𝔣𝔢

BENEDICTO BENEDICATUR

O years! and Age! Farewell;
  Behold I go,
  Where I do know
Infinity to dwell.

And these mine eyes shall see
  All times, how they
  Are lost i' the Sea
Of vast Eternity.
                    ROBERT HERRICK.

THE request to write a paper on the future life comes to me somewhat un-
expectedly, as did once a sudden invitation
to say grace at the dinner-table of a lady
who had invited me to give a literary lecture
to her school, a large and celebrated one in
the western part of Massachusetts. It was
many years since I had been asked to do
such a thing, but there came into my memory

two words which an American visitor finds
so impressive at a certain college dining-hall
at Oxford: "Benedicto benedicatur" ("Blessings to the Blessed One"). I said this grace,
and on sitting down afterward on the right
hand of my hostess, I remember to have
glanced at her with some slight misgiving,
and she looked at me with an expression of
radiant delight. Then she said that I could
not possibly have said a grace which would
have impressed her so much, for she had
previously heard it as a guest at an Oxford
University table and it seemed to her that
she never had heard so much put into two
words. She felt it so greatly, indeed, that
she took me into the chapel of the institution
at morning service, the next day, and after
her prayers in the presence of the students
were over, she invited me to say something
to them, though she knew me to be somewhat of a heretic. This was the outcome of
a grace learned by myself at Oxford, and I
take it as a motto for what I have to say.

In the wondrous description given by Plato
of the last days of Socrates, the latter's friend
Crito is described as asking him the ques-

tion, since repeated so many million times by others, "How and where shall we bury you?" Socrates rebukes the phrase instantly. "Bury me," he answers, "in any way you please, if you can catch me to bury," "he at the same time smiling and looking gently round upon us," says Plato, his biographer. "I cannot persuade Crito, my friends," Socrates adds, "that I am the Socrates who is now conversing with you and arranging each part of this discourse; but he obstinately thinks I am that which he shall shortly behold dead, and he wants to know how he shall bury me. But that which I have been arguing to you so long—that when I have drunk this poison I shall be with you no longer, but shall depart straightway to some happy state of the blessed—this I cannot convince him." "Say rather, Crito," he urges, pleadingly, once more—"say, if you love me, Where shall you bury my body? and I will answer you, Bury it in any manner and in any place you please."

Many centuries have passed since then; sects and sages, faiths and governments, have come and gone. The world is taken captive by a religion unknown to Socrates; yet still through Christendom the words of the great ancient philosopher survive; and with them the words of his faithless questioner linger also, and for one who speaks like Socrates to-day, a thousand even in Christendom speak like Crito. The habitual forms and words of Christendom show this practical faithlessness to the spiritual life it claims to monopolize. We drape our houses and our persons in gloomy black, beneath its influence; and leave white to the pagan Chinese, and purple and golden hues to the heathen Greeks and Romans. It is centuries since Saint Charles Borromeo strove to substitute for the skeleton and the scythe the golden key of paradise; and yet the skeleton is still the symbol of death, and the scythe of terror.

I speak as one reared on the vanishing edge, as it were, of the old Calvinistic faith, so as just to miss its gloomy training. My father, though a man of secular pursuits, was the first organizer of the Harvard Theological School, now thoroughly liberalized and always looking in that direction. My mother, though reading more successive volumes of sermons than any one I ever knew, was a liberal Unitarian, said grace at the dinner-table, and held family prayers. We were allowed to play games on Sunday evening, but they were cards of what was then called "sacred geography," and I learned from them, once for all, that the capital of Dahomey was Abomey, which, indeed, became a saying in the family. I say these things because we are called upon to speak of personal experiences as well as personal opinions.

After these mild beginnings, I may frankly say that I never consciously at any period in my youth technically performed any process called "experiencing religion." What I did have the opportunity to appreciate, however, was the society of saints at home and sinners abroad, and, above all, the fact of certain very extraordinary cases of persons, intimately known to me, who underwent great and prolonged trials and sorrows without especial religious consolation. I was also born just in time to meet the strong influences of Emerson, Parker, and Garrison. I walked in their paths and have never regretted it. All this was somewhat exceptional in those restricted days, whereas I now see around me on every side a generation to whom religion represents something liberal and cheering, not merely technical. This is accompanied, however, by new problems of thought, perhaps harder than any which have preceded them. Living as I do next door to a Catholic church whose thronged aisles and schools are heartily to be respected, I look over it to the high grounds of the Harvard Observatory, whence has just come to us within a few days the announcement of the discovery of a new-found planet in the solar system, farther off than any previously known, and so far that it will probably never be seen by the naked eye or even through the telescope, but only demonstrable through the eyes of abstract science. To the power which creates in the universe such inscrutable wonders what better can one say than "Benedicto benedicatur"?

But the past is one thing, the present is another. Within my memory the early Colonial expressions of religion have largely gone out of use, and the changed utterances of the present have taken their place. How largely, for instance, have the old habits of family prayers diminished, or even that of saying grace at private tables. Is this because there is no more need of them? Quite otherwise! Who is there who can go through the sorrows and bereavements of mortal life without days of anxiety and grief, perhaps even nights of tears? These may be periods in which there comes at length into the soul, even if only temporarily, a recognition, not merely of a Deity, but of a God close by, so near as to need no intermediate aid. At such a moment do not all sects and creeds suddenly become valueless to us, and personal immortality seem as sure as to-morrow's sunrise? We have, in the Scripture phrase, gone into the closet and shut the door. At such a moment we do not, it may be, need an uttered word, or if we are to have it, it must be neither technical nor conventional. Some simple poem of Whittier, perhaps, some verse which the hymn-books have borrowed from him and with a few daring touches have made their own, these give more than any Church ritual can offer, and we turn to a simple book like John Woolman's *Journal* without caring for Church forms.

But we are compelled to bear in mind the fact that beyond these personal experiences there is a world of religious imaginings, excitements, ordeals, which when once endured are not easily disposed of. More often they remain in the field. We speak of the excesses of spiritualism, for instance, as something gone by. But there lies before me a letter of twelve quarto pages from an educated family in the Far West, some of whom are personally known to me, and whose respective houses are to this day filled with unexplained "sweet - bell - sounds," or "chimes," as they describe them, sometimes thirty in a single day. These oftentimes chimed so easily with words, that by automatic writing, messages from the departed could be taken down and have a coherent meaning. At other times they seemed to ring in approval of some statement that had been made. The bell - ringing is described in one of these curious letters as follows:

"Mother told me of hearing the bell 107 times when she was alone. She and I heard

it 28 times. Mother, Joseph, & I heard it
once. Mary & I heard it twice. The four
of us heard the sounds five times. Mother &
Mary S. . . . heard it once. Mother and
Mary T. . . . heard it seven times. . . . Mother,
Mary, & Joseph heard it six times. . . . I
heard the bell 71 times when I was alone; 42
of those sounds were in my room a couple of
blocks away"; and so on indefinitely. All
this occurred, it will be observed, not to
single hearers only, but to groups of different members of a large family, and all this
at different localities, several blocks of houses
apart.

These and similar unexplained phenomena
bring happiness to those who believe that they
are messages from the spirit world; while
to more prosaic minds they seem imaginary or uncanny. At any rate, this is one
side. Observe, on the other hand, what a
change has come over the habits of the cul-
tivated mind in its view of the Hebrew and
Christian Scriptures. "The general religious
world," says one of the highest scientific authorities, Sir Oliver Lodge, President of the
University of Birmingham, "has agreed ap-

parently to throw overboard Jonah and the whale, Joshua and the sun, the three Children and the fiery furnace; it does not seem to take anything in the Book of Judges or the Book of Daniel very seriously; . . . it is willing to relegate to poetry—*i.e.*, to imagination or fiction—such legends as the creation of the world, Adam and his rib, Eve and the apple, Noah and his ark, language and the tower of Babel, Elijah and the chariot of fire, and many others." But he justly asks "if religious people go as far as this, where are they to stop? What, then, do they propose to do with the turning of water into wine, the ejection of devils, the cursing of the fig-tree, the feeding of five thousand, the raising of Lazarus?" [1] to say nothing of wonders greater still which are evaded even by so liberal a man as Dr. Lyman Abbott. Yet science teaches us more and more unflinchingly that there has been no such thing in history as the fall of man, in the accustomed sense. It is tracing him, or claims to be, back through a tadpole and fish-like an-

[1] Lodge's *Science and Immortality*, 13, 14.

cestry away to the early beginnings of existence, but it has not been able to trace the
origin of any portion of such life from dead
matter. Perpetual efforts have been made
by the most learned of modern men to reach
the beginning of animal life; claims have
been made more than once to have absolutely created it. In Germany, we are told
"inorganic and artificial substances have
been found to crawl about on glass slides
under the action of surface-tension or capil-
larity, with an appearance which is said to
have deceived even a biologist."[1] We are
told that there is not such a student but believes that sooner or later the discovery will
be made, and that a cell having all the essential functions of life will be constructed
out of inorganic material. So vast has been
the progress of chemistry that within sev-
enty years the very word has lost its meaning
and has advanced to deeper and more difficult properties. Profounder and profounder
knowledge carries us far away from many
an old tradition, but it still leaves untouched

---

[1] Lodge's *Science and Immortality*, 18.

145

the instinct which convinces us that there is a God. The poetic side exists as strongly and keeps as near to us as what is called philosophy. Whittier's simple phrases carry us no farther than that song sung by Emily Brontë on her death-bed:

"Though earth and man were gone
  And suns and universe ceased to be
And Thou were left alone,
  Every existence would exist in Thee."

This is matched by the profounder eloquence of Carlyle:

"What, then, is man? What, then, is man!"

"He endures but for an hour, and is crushed before the moth. Yet in the being and in the working of a faithful man is there already (as all faith from the beginning gives assurance) a something that pertains not to this wild death-element of Time; that triumphs over Time, and *is*, and will be, when Time shall be no more." [1]

[1] Lodge's *Science and Immortality*, 161.

There lies before me a letter from that faithful friend of truth, Elizabeth Peabody, well-known as the source and founder in America of the kindergarten system. This letter, never before published, seems to me to touch the whole subject of human bereavement more profoundly than anything else I know.

"MY DEAR ——,—I must write to tell you how very much grieved I was to see in the paper to-day (but it was an old one) that you had lost your little darling in whose advent & welcome all your friends have so rejoiced with you.

"I have sympathized with many parents as only one can who looks on childhood as I do. It is a terrible pang for a parent to have the angel presence withdrawn so soon. But in a Father's House we know that it is not without its other side— whatever happens—Just now you are I dare say in the mood of Emerson's wail in the Threnody— Do you know that it was quite at first he poured out that song of woe— & it was not till a year afterward he wrote the rest—from the words 'The Deep Heart replied'—This fact gives both parts more meaning—and I think you will find solace in reading just now the first part & then thinking of the rich consolation & instruction in store for you—You may be more to your race for going down into these mysterious depths. It is death which reveals the infinite sweetness of life 'with the might of his sunbeams touching the day.' . . .

"I believe the mother here [on earth] can bless & develop it if she be true to her motherly love. It is an infinite tie—As the life of the Angel expands, it must look with more and more gratitude upon the loving parents who invoked it from the bosom of God to personal consciousness.

"But excuse me for making suggestions when God has spoken to you so intimately—'As a Mother comforts her little one—so I comfort thee' saith the Lord—

"Your friend,
"ELIZ. P. PEABODY.

"Concord, Mass—
"*March* 20 [1880]"

Strange indeed it is that the simple belief in immortality, so plain to Socrates and Cicero, should have become confused and bewildered in spite of those later religious teachings which would seem to make it sure. One of the most devoted mothers whom I ever knew, an eminent literary woman, when her elder children had died and when her husband, a distinguished army officer, followed them suddenly, devoted herself absorbingly to her remaining boy, a child of eight or ten, of uncommonly mature character. When he was ill, these two entered into the most solemn pledges with each other that either of them which died first should, if it were possible, speak to the other in some form. The boy died and she listened during her lifetime, but heard nothing. No one can count the number of cases in which the same thing may have been attempted in vain. "Neither philosophy nor science has added in countless ages," says a brilliant modern writer, "a single demonstration of another life, nor faith nor pious supplication brought back one soul to tell us of our heaven."

On the other hand, how many noble souls unconsciously predict that heaven before they die? How many experiences we have, as we grow older, even among our own kindred, of lives that may be called heavenly in their very dying. Of a dearly loved cousin of mine, in Virginia, her daughter lately wrote: "On yesterday, at 2.30 P.M., my wonderful mother passed into the beyond. She retained her faculties up to three minutes before death, and the same old seraphic smile, familiar to you, I know, came over her features and it was all over."

Still more striking was the death of a young woman who was engaged to a friend of mine, and who went out of this life with such superb faith in the beyond that the manner of her going is still—after a lapse of many years—an inspiring memory. She died of consumption, of which dread disease her father, brother, and two sisters had already been the victims. She sat in a great old-fashioned easy-chair, her hand clasped in that of her lover, while her mother and remaining sisters hovered anxiously about, though she herself remained perfectly conscious and calm. Occasionally her face lighted up with what seemed a radiance from another world, and her eyes shone with a mysterious joy, as if she saw something invisible to the others. From this half-translated state she would return from time to time to her familiar surroundings, when again the vision would enthrall her; and while her face was thus transfigured, the end came.

The same unconscious testimony lasts after death. Of my own mother, I can say that I never saw her beautiful face so calm and so full of deferred utterance as when I sat alone beside it after death; it was of itself a lesson in immortality—the very lesson implied in that fine saying of Swedenborg that "in heaven the angels are advancing continually to the springtime of their youth, so that the oldest angel appears the youngest."

I know at least one woman poet who has strengthened my faith and expressed her own by this poem which has already comforted many hearts:

IN THE DARK

The fields were silent, and the woodland drear;
   The moon had set, and clouds hid all the stars;
And blindly, when a footfall met my ear,
   I reached across the bars.

And swift as thought this hand was clasped in thine,
   Though darkness hung around us and above;
Not guided by uncertain fate to mine,
   But by the law of love.

151

In After Days

I know not which of us may first go hence
    And leave the other to be brave alone,
Unable to dispel the shadows dense
    That veil the life unknown;

But if I linger last, and stretch once more
    A longing hand, when fades this earthly day,
Again it will be grasped by thine, before
    My steps can lose the way.

WILLIAM HANNA THOMSON

The Future State
William Hanna Thomson, M. D.

VII

The Future State

NOT unlike one of Fontaine's fables is the story of three small ants who, as they gathered on the dry leaf of a tree overhanging a swiftly flowing river, the leaf loosened and was soon carrying them floating on the water. After a brief consultation each of the ants went to inspect one side of the leaf, and the collective report was that no land was to be seen on either side, but only moving water everywhere. Suddenly the leaf turned round and round in a way which the ants could in no wise prevent, for it had fallen into a little whirlpool and alarmed them by getting its hitherto dry surface wet. One of the ants then thought that he could get a wider view than his fellows by ascending the upturned stem of the leaf, and thence see what he could see. He espied a number of bubbles on the surface of the water and a large one of bright colors coming in contact with the edge of the leaf. Down he sped to take passage on this bubble, only to find that it could not bear the weight of one little ant, but forthwith disappeared and himself with it.

Such are we also upon the swiftly passing stream of our life. We scarcely know how we happened to be so placed, nor where the river is to take us; but we do know that the thing which carries us is very frail, and at any time may go under. What by this time we ought to know, also, is that we should not commit ourselves to any bubble of human speculation. Such bubbles float about us in plenty, but after so many of them have been tested, our reason should tell us not to rely on the guesses of our fellows, who at their best cannot see much farther than we can see, but to seek rather to attach ourselves only to historic fact. For whatever has once been historic remains always historic, unchanged by the winds, the currents, and the storms of the centuries. Therefore, the only way to deal with what claims to be historic is not to speculate about it, but to find whether it happened or not.

Now the Christian religion is nothing unless it be historical, because, as St. Paul justly says, it is so based on the historical event of the Resurrection of our Lord Jesus Christ, that if that Resurrection did not occur, the Christian faith is vain and nothing but the emptiest of delusions. We cannot appreciate this truth too deeply, for without the Resurrection, Death is still the Victor, and there can be no Christian religion nor Christian hope.

But whatever is asserted to be a historical event must be judged by the rules of historical evidence, especially if, as in the case of the Resurrection, a length of time has elapsed since its occurrence. Therefore, that event, above all others, must be supported by the testimony of a number and a variety of witnesses. Its effects also on those witnesses should be the same as we would look for on sober persons in our time if a like event happened to them. Then if the event itself was so important that it would vitally affect the history of the world, the subsequent history of the world should show it. There is no escaping *that* conclusion, and we may say here that this is a test which no Christian need fear. For there has been nothing like the belief in the Resurrection for making history, recording both great triumphs and great setbacks for the Church. The unavailing persecutions of the Roman emperors, followed as they were by the great disaster of the conversion of Constantine, from the evils of which the Church has by no means yet recovered, the mighty struggle of the Crusaders for possession of the Sepulchre of the Resurrection, and particularly modern Christendom itself, nineteen centuries after the Resurrection, bear no resemblance to speculations or to theories, but are great historic facts, with the Cross and the Triumph over Death above them all.

The night before His death, our Lord, while walking to Gethsemane, said to His disciples, "Apart from Me ye can do nothing!" According to all precedents the separation of death was soon to sunder Him from them as completely as death can part. Soon those disciples themselves all forsook Him and fled. But afterward those same frightened men, though seemingly quite apart from Him, calmly faced high priests, governors, and kings, as their Master foretold that they would. They themselves explain what wrought this great change in them—namely, that they had seen their Lord, who had died, alive again. We would be equally changed by such an experience. If a dear friend of ours whom we had seen die, and then buried before our eyes, should appear again to us unmistakably alive, and so converse with us, our whole thought about the next world would be wholly changed. If we were sound and true men this world and everything in it would then sink into insignificance.

Nor can this story, which was accompanied by such intense personal conviction, be explained away as one of those myths which not infrequently have grown up about a remarkable historical figure. Myths take time to grow, but long before any of the Gospel narratives was composed, St. Paul wrote the chapter xv of I. Corinthians, in which he says that one and another, and then the Twelve, and then above five hundred men,

159

at once saw the risen Lord, of whom the greater part were still living witnesses when he wrote; and last of all he himself saw and spoke with Jesus, with the result that he was never the same man again, and instead of hating Jesus he lived only for Him until he bowed his head to the axe.

As a medical man myself, I have long been professionally acquainted with the phenomena of illusions and hallucinations. But I have never known them to last with sane persons, and least of all to have such persons risk their lives in asserting them. Illusions and hallucinations change nothing for long. At the most they are but passing gusts of wind and never could deposit the solid strata which history is made of.

But if we attach ourselves to historic fact, our confidence should increase in proportion as we note to what supreme truths this fact is taking us. And so with the Resurrection as its corner-stone, Personality becomes all in all to Christianity, and thus separates it from all other religions, which connect the future state not so much with personality as with place. Most persons even now try to picture what sort of place heaven is, and so they have recourse to the imagination, that most earthly of our faculties because it cannot make one of its pictures except out of materials furnished by earthly experience. Hence the essential sameness in all human conceptions of the other world. The old Egyptian depicted an ideal Egypt beyond, with Egyptian good things rewarding the virtuous. The Greek had his Elysian Fields, and the American Indian his happy hunting-grounds. Mohammed's paradise, however, gives the fullest details of future bodily delights which would excite the Arab imagination. Having lived during my youth among Mohammedans, I can say that nothing could so destroy everything good in human nature as a desire for the Moslem's future state. So revolting and purely sensual is it throughout, that we should be thankful that Moses refrained altogether from mentioning the next world to his Hebrews. They are the Shemitic cousins to the Arabs, and if in the formative stage in which they were then, their great lawgiver had given a hint of a future world, inevitably would they have pictured it to themselves as an eternal abode of animalism. Instead, after the one awe-inspiring lesson of Sinai, that their God is the Holy and Righteous One, a lesson which forever kept them even when most inclined to idolatry, just as it has kept Europeans and Americans since, from ever *confounding* Jehovah with the gods of the heathen, Moses then simply enjoined religion as the best thing for this life.

A great principle appears here, which is that God's revelations are always conditioned by human receptivity.

But as the centuries of spiritual education rolled on, devout men had to explain to themselves why, though Moses' promise of present reward to those who lived a righteous life was true as a general principle, it was altogether wanting when applied to individuals. In the actual world in which they lived they saw men choosing murder as the chief means for political advancement, and profiting thereby. While such wicked men enjoyed every worldly prosperity, many righteous met with nothing but adversity. It is most instructive to note how often this painful perplexity tried

162

the souls of the great psalmists, but also how in every case it finally led them to the conviction of another world to come. What that world is to be they state in terms as clear and as beautiful as we find in any references to that subject in the New Testament.

The reader should compare (in the Revised Version) Ps. xvi; Ps. xvii; Ps. xxiii; Ps. xxxvii, 37; Ps. lxxiii, 23–24.

In the New Testament, on the other hand, apart from what is related about Christ Himself in the interval between His Resurrection and His Ascension, there is only one passage which gives us any item of information about heaven, and that is in the account of the Transfiguration. From it we learn the precious truth of personal recognition and abiding individuality, because Moses and Elijah were the same persons then that they were when they lived on the earth.

In the book of Revelation it is impossible for human curiosity to penetrate through its thick veil of metaphor to discern any of the circumstances, as they may be called, of heaven. It begins with a picture of seven golden lamp-stands brightly lighted. They

163

are seven Christian churches in places of thick darkness. It ends with a vision of a great city built entirely of precious stones and with gates of pearl. But this heavenly city turns out to be a great society of perfected human persons, because it is the Church and also the Bride of the Lamb.

But in that chapter of I. Corinthians, which, as we have stated, is chronologically one of the earliest parts of the New Testament, and which was written after the date of the Resurrection at a less interval than that which separates us from the first term, as President, of Mr. Cleveland, Paul tells us more about the future state than we find in any other one passage in the Bible. We are to have bodies, but they are to be bodies which shall be free from flesh and blood forever. As there is no grown human body which is not composed of flesh and blood, Paul's resurrection body must be very different from anything we see here. He, therefore, soon hears one asking how such a thing could be. Paul answers by an appeal to the greatest mystery in the living world—a seed. But he could not have imagined then how immeasurably modern science has strengthened the force of that appeal. The completest of all whales is one of whom 1,500,000 such whales could be gathered into the space occupied by a pin's head. He has then only one cell to his physical being, but that cell is a whale and nothing but a whale, and cannot possibly grow into a fish any more than it can grow into a bird, for whales are mammals and hence separated by an impassable biological gulf from all fishes. Long before it has either flesh or blood, that microscopic dot is a whale's own body sure enough, because from it alone are to grow the billions of cells of the adult whale's body, each of them fashioned after the specific pattern of the first cell. Moreover, in that first cell is the indelible hereditary impress of the whale's ancestors back to the first whale.

Therefore, Paul's argument, as we at present can state it, is that already a living body goes through the most marvellous changes without breaking its continuity with the body preceding it. That is because there is in it a living agency which is never the same with the physical materials which it moulds, any more than an architect is the same with the stones of the building which he erects. Those earthly materials are constantly being changed and cast aside by that invisible architect which uses the materials as a temporary dress, and no more. Therefore, cannot the Almighty, the Source of Life, clothe this the real body with the new garment of the risen body? He can, for the seed sown in weakness here will develop into the new body endowed with power, imperishable and glorious like the body of the Lord Man from Heaven.

Instead, therefore, of a Greek hades, peopled by thin shades and ghosts, our heaven will show the dear features and lineaments of our departed so vividly that then for the first time we will know what life is. Here on earth, owing to the easy exhaustion of our mortal bodies, we lose one-third of our lives in sleep, and many of our waking hours we pass but little better than in a dream. But there it will be fulness of life for evermore. We need not then ask what our surroundings will be, for even on this poor earth a place is a garden or a desert according to those

who live there. The promised eternal life
is not to be mere existence, for what is life
here without society with interchange of life
with other living, active minds, hearts, and
wills ? We should, therefore, not ask where
we are to be, but with *whom* we are to be in
the world beyond.

Many Christians are disturbed, if not
shaken, at the rejection, by eminent men of
the world, of our divine revelation, and particularly by the falling away of so many
from the faith of their fathers. But both
these events in the future were repeatedly
and explicitly foretold by our Lord and by
His inspired apostles. They are all due to
that deep unceasing antagonism of human
nature, whose central motive is self and self-
approval, to that new nature which the Holy
Spirit alone can give, whose central motive
is the all-searching principle of self-sacrifice,
and of which Christ Himself is the greatest
example. But again let us turn to historical
fact. The end of every century since the
Resurrection has shown more believers in
Christ than at its beginning. Voltaire boasted that it took twelve men to found the

Christian Church, but it needed only one, himself, to overturn it. That was at the end of the eighteenth century. Now, at the end of the nineteenth century, there are at least five to one, compared with Voltaire's time, whose faith rests upon the Risen One.

The store which other religions put upon place in their conceptions of the future state shows how superficial they all are. In them the surroundings of self are more thought of than the self which is the centric fact of all. For human personality not only includes mind, but also feeling, disposition, and will; in other words, it is we as we are indeed. Personality is itself indestructible. Whatever part of the physical body be cut off, whether hand or foot, no part of the personality goes with it. Modern medical science also proves that the brain does not itself think, but is only the instrument of the invisible thinker, just as the hand is. Personality is also our certainty of certainties. Whatever the case may be with what is outside of us, whether that be reality or only appearance, we inwardly are sure that we exist.

This is all in full accord with the statement, repeated five times for emphasis, when man is first spoken of in the Bible, that in man we are to see the image and likeness of God. When Moses asked God what His name is, the answer was, "My Name is—I am!" That is also what man can say, I am! and never to better purpose than when he is thinking deeply about himself, about this world, and about the world which is to come, for then he can discern in himself these true likenesses to his Father.

1. Man knows that he himself is invisible. No one can tell what he thinks or purposes within, unless he chooses to reveal himself, and, like God, he does not often reveal himself except to those who sympathize with him.

2. However he may change in his body during his years, man remains the same personality and never becomes any one else, so that he can truly say that he is the same yesterday as to-day, and, therefore, he will be the same hereafter.

3. Alone of all beings on earth, man knows what law is, and that it is eternal and omnipresent, ruling not only the material but also

169

the intelligent universe. Well, therefore, did the old Psalmist exclaim, as he recognized the majesty before him of judges in their seats, "I said ye are *Elohim* (God) and every one of you sons of the Most High! But if they forget this they would die like men" (Ps. lxxxii, 6). There is no race of man, from the highest to the lowest, that does not know what the word justice means.

4. But man also reflects in himself the Infinite. He does not know the word enough by experience, but insatiably asks for more, whether it be possession, power, or attainment. He is therefore equipped for a boundless existence. Could I ever cease wanting to know more?

5. But man is as true a creator as God Himself is, for a creator is one who gives origin to things which would not otherwise exist but for his intelligent purpose and design. On that account the whole earth is full of things which man and not God has created. And what marvels many of those human creations are, showing what a master man is of both matter and force! How little does this earth now resemble what it was be-

fore man took it in hand! And all this is done while his stay here is so brief. If only he had time, time never cut short by death, what would he accomplish!

Such a being is of immeasurable worth. Value is a term which cannot be connected with anything impersonal. What is the value of the great antarctic continent if no one can live there? So a universe of matter is of no more value than empty space if it be of nothing but matter. Some speak of this earth as being such an insignificant speck among the starry worlds, that man must share in his world's insignificance. But as those worlds are so largely composed of burning hydrogen gas, how much hydrogen gas will it take to become valuable without a sentient being to make use of it? The truth is that it is *matter* which is insignificant compared with one imperishable human mind.

But there is a perfectability in man, the thought of which deeply stirs the heart. This was shown by men in the darkest days of the Old Testament when, without a clear revelation of the Rest beyond, they nevertheless faced a cruel death rather than deny God.

To appreciate poetry we should fully understand the poet's allusions. The xlii.-iii. psalms (one psalm) was composed by a poor Hebrew captive as he was driven past Mt. Hermon in winter on his way to Babylon. Of the thirty-three peoples which Tiglath Pileser says he caused to undergo that terrible ordeal of captivity, not one survived it. Little, but abiding, Judah survived the captivity, though this psalmist had witnessed the hideous spectacle of infants' heads dashed by brutal soldiers against the stones lest they would encumber the march. The psalmist's earliest journey had been with his parents—and who does not vividly remember such early journeys—to go up to the House of the Lord, and three times a year since he had joined in such pilgrimage to listen to the splendid antiphonies of Ps. cxviii, 19–29, from the battlements of the Temple and the answers of the approaching multitude keeping holy day. But now he was like the thirsty hart which dreads to approach the water-brooks because it well knows that lions are waiting there for it. No sight in nature ever impressed me (the writer) as a

storm on the slopes near Mt. Hermon when
four waterspouts rose simultaneously from
the darkened Mediterranean to the black
cloud which stretched for a hundred miles
over the sea, as it approached the great
mountain range. Incessant lightning, with
thunder which echoed through the valleys,
caused our horses to tremble under us as
the mighty phalanx of clouds drew near.
"Deep calleth unto deep at the noise of Thy
waterspouts; all Thy waves and Thy billows
have gone over me." But worst of all, "as
with a sword in my bones, mine enemies reproach me, while they continually say unto
me, where is thy god?" According to all
then accepted standards Jehovah had failed.
He could not protect His own people from
the bitterest of calamities, nor even His Temple, for the Ark and the golden vessels were
being carried by the heathen to put in triumph before the image of their mightier
Merodach. But as each fresh recollection
brought its anguish, this man could answer
with that beautiful refrain, "Why art thou
cast down, O my soul, and why art thou
disquieted within me? Hope thou in God,

for I shall yet praise Him who is the health of my countenance and my God!" In comparison with Christians in these days of light, being disquieted at the ranks of unbelievers, what was this man's faith? Probably no archangel in heaven was ever subjected to such a test of loyalty to God as was this mourning captive. Heart preference being the deepest test of character, we now can understand what justification by faith means, and that it will be the special honor through eternity of the redeemed children of men.

I am now an old man, and five times have I stood at an open grave to see it close over the remains of my own beloved. The associations connected with such experiences are too sacred for public mention or reference. It is only because I have been asked to write some words for the comfort of other bereaved ones that I do so now. An open grave is a cold and dark place. Vainly have I sought in human science or philosophy for a ray of light to dispel that darkness. There in our desolation and utter helplessness we do not ask for doctrine, not even for the doctrine of the Resurrection. We long for the presence of a mighty Friend. And as such He comes with His unmistakable personal voice saying, "*I* am the Resurrection and the Life. Whosoever believeth in *Me* shall never die." That is also in keeping with what Paul said as he approached his last day. I *know*—not what I believed—but *whom* I have believed. So when stricken ones turn to leave their scene of burial let them think of that inspired word. "For if we believe that Jesus died and rose again, even so those also that are fallen asleep in Jesus will God bring with Him." What will that Reunion be! Our loved ones are given us here for us to learn and know in advance Him whose name is Love. How plainly we are told that we shall do so because we shall be then in His likeness. When the beloved Apostle wrote, "Now are we the sons of God, and it doth not yet appear what we shall be: but we know that when He shall appear we shall be like Him, for we shall see Him as He is," he was but echoing the words of the old Psalmist, "As for me, I shall be satisfied when I awake in Thy likeness."

175

GUGLIELMO FERRERO

The Life After This
Guglielmo Ferrero

VIII

𝔗𝔥𝔢 𝔏𝔦𝔣𝔢 𝔄𝔣𝔱𝔢𝔯 𝔗𝔥𝔦𝔰

"Qui fit, Mæcenas, ut nemo, quam sibi sortem
Seu ratio dederit, seu fors obiecerit, illa
Contentus vivat; laudet diversa sequentes?" . . .

"Why, O Mæcenas, is no one content with his
lot, whether it be chosen by himself or thrust
upon him by fate, but praises those that follow other callings? 'O fortunate merchants!'
cries the soldier, burdened with years and broken
with much labor. The merchant in his turn, while
his ships are buffeted by the winds, declares the
soldiers' life the better. And why? Hand to
hand they fight; in a moment comes swift death
or happy victory. The lawyer praises the farmer,
when at cockcrow the client knocks at his door.
The countryman, come to the city on summons
from court, declares only the city-dweller happy."

SO it was in the days of the greatest splendor
of Rome, when the civil wars were ended
and the city was on the point of uniting and

179

enjoying, under a sceptre of peace, the vast empire conquered by three centuries of fortunate wars; so its great poet, Horace, voiced the universal discontent, the restless dissatisfaction of all. Who does not see that these verses might be with equal truth repeated of our own times, in the refulgence of wealth, of power, of glory, of knowledge, that enlightens modern civilization? Men have never been so rich, so powerful, so clever, as they now are; nor have they ever been so discontented, so anxious for change, the prey of so intemperate a mania to find new homes, different occupations, fresh experiences of life. To how many of us will befall the lot of being laid to rest for the eternal sleep in the village or the city where our eyes first saw the sun? Almost no man is disposed to carry on the profession of his father; the new generation seems always bent upon beginning over again; everybody changes from one study to another, from one profession to another, impelled by the continuous need of seeking a perfection, a greater happiness, an ideal ever vanishing, which, ever deluding our hopes and expectations, is the supreme torment of our lives.

This is exactly the same state of things as existed in the time of Horace, and for the same reasons. Riches, power, knowledge, do not increase our happiness, just as they did not increase it for the contemporaries of the great poet of Venosa; for we also, like the Romans of the period of Augustus, place the end of living too much within ourselves. We lose faith in those ideas and beliefs that propose to man an aim outside himself, beyond his own personal interests and pleasures and the time in which he lives—ideals that sometimes cause him to sacrifice to this high end his own interests, his personal pleasures, and even the brief moment of time that is to him the whole patrimony of life. These ideals, these beliefs, are chiefly three: glory, family, and a future life.

If there be a sentiment that has almost entirely disappeared from the mind of the modern man, it is the solicitude for the good opinion of posterity. Among the ancients, on the contrary, at least in certain epochs in the history of the Greeks and Romans, how vivid was this feeling! The admiration of posterity, the perpetuation of one's own name—in a word, immortality—was then a need among minds elect, an obligation in great families: to satisfy this need, to maintain this obligation, individuals and families often cheerfully suffered exile, persecution, ruin, and even death. Man lived spiritually almost in contact with future generations. Religion, tradition, literature, all fed this ardent hunger for immortality among choice spirits. To-day they do it no more: statesmen, writers, philosophers, artists, athletes, all are anxious to know, not what the world will think of them in the twenty-first and twenty-second centuries, but what the newspaper with the largest number of readers will say of them the next day. The present, with its struggles, its passions, its urgencies, and its multiple seductions, quite bars out our vision of what is to come. No civilization has considered the future less than our own has done, and no age has therefore been less able to enjoy the comforts that absorbing interest in a future life can give to man.

The longing for immortality as expressed

in the attainment of glory can be comfort
and stimulus to but a small minority—the
minority made up of men singularly gifted,
and of aristocratic families already habitu-
ated to the power and wealth secured by
preceding generations. The vast majority
are necessarily shut out from winning great
distinction, because only a few in every generation can reasonably hope to survive for
centuries in the memory of posterity. In
fact, this passion for glory is found only in
intellectual or political aristocracies.

The cult of ancestors, on the other hand,
the religion of family, as known by ancient
Greeks and Romans and practised to-day in
China, can give the joys of a more restricted
immortality to all who, among the events of
common existence, succeed in founding and
continuing a family for several generations.
Then a man knows that, although all the
efforts put forth by him to preserve and
augment the material fortune and the reputation of the family—his own laboriousness,
his spirit of self-abnegation, his sufferings—
will bring to him in person but transitory
recompense upon the earth, the greatest re-

ward will come after death; then, for his own children, he will be transformed into a god, and as such will be venerated and invoked by them; then, without further pain or trouble, he will enjoy the complete devotion of his descendants, and without risk or fatigue to himself can return their worship by doing them good as the guardian spirit of their daily affairs.

Who in the European-American civilization holds this faith to-day? Not only the transformation of our ideas in regard to the spiritual principle of man makes it difficult for us to conceive the *Manes* to whom the Romans rendered homage, or the souls of ancestors whom the Chinese so piously venerate; but more, the dissolution of the family extinguishes the sentiment from which that cult is born and developed. Children grow up to-day with ideas too different from those of their parents, and detach themselves too soon from the family that has educated them. Europe and America seem destined to be covered by an infinite number of separate hearth-fires, each too small to outlast a generation, and their indifferent builders can neither believe in their own immortality nor find in such an ideal a force and serenity that shall illumine their daily affairs. At the cost of great effort the modern age succeeds in saving that last material relic of the ancient cult of family—the religion of the tomb. But for how long? Will the sons who love their parents be able much longer to bury them among flowers and heap upon their graves the memorial signs of filial affection? I fear that one day or other some hygienist will invent a machine or a process utterly and instantly to destroy the body, and that the practical spirit of years to come will decide to spare the expense of cemeteries. Who does not know that land in modern cities is extravagantly dear? The lodging of the dead costs too much.

So much the more ought men to take refuge in the belief in the future life—this immortality opened to all, even the poorest and the simplest; not only to him who will never succeed in making his own name famous in some grand empire, but also to him who can never found a family. The belief in the future life, if it do not altogether die out, instead of gaining ground, is becoming to many minds a thing as vague, indefinite, and colorless as it was to the contemporaries of Horace; it can then no more sustain and console men in annoyance and adversity. Perhaps the doctrines in which this belief has taken shape no longer suit the changed conditions of men's minds, and new teachings able to replace them have not been yet formulated. Perhaps modern life too much absorbs and fatigues the spirit, insisting that every man, even he of humble circumstances, shall learn and do too many things; so that he has neither the leisure nor the will to test ideals, and, sounding them, to stir his imagination till it transform them into something more precious and important than the guise in which they first appeared. Modern men are proud of their activity; but the too active life spurns the contemplative, atrophies the imagination, habituates the spirit to heeding only concrete things.

From this extinguishing of the ideal passions, this failing of the imagination, this obliterating of the beliefs that put to life some end beyond the material, is born the trouble, the malcontent, and the pessimism of our day, like that which tormented the times of Horace.

> "L'homme est un puits où le vide toujours Recommence,"

wrote Victor Hugo. There is nothing to-day more unreasonable than the bitter envy with which so many look upon others who seem to possess those supreme gifts of life, wealth and power. Feeling themselves unhappy or discontented, most men attribute their state to a want of material means, or to the little power at their command. It does not occur to them that two centuries ago men in their relative condition had less wealth and no power, yet complained far less than we; that the matter is plainly and solely envy.

In fact, we live in a time when riches and power have little weight in producing happiness, and, therefore, are of relatively little value, because men are too anxious for them and forget everything else for them.

"Oui, de leur sort tous les hommes sont las,
Pour être heureux à tous—destin morose!
Tout a manqué. Tout, c'est à dire, hélas,
Peu de chose."

Again I quote Victor Hugo. The *peu de chose* that fails us is precisely a desire, strong and sure, for something unattainable in this life. Man cannot be happy unless he ardently longs for and awaits with assurance —which is more difficult than the longing— something he will not be able to obtain while he lives, be it immortal glory, or the loving cult of surviving children, or the paradise splendors of an eternity yonder; unless he projects beyond the span of his own life a vital part of his aspirations and invests them with his living spiritual forces. If all his desires be fully circumscribed by the time in which he lives, what happens to a man? On the one hand, he strains himself desperately to satisfy them, without relaxing for a moment of respite, worrying over his unsuccesses and jealous of his more fortunate rivals. Who will be able to compensate him for what he has not possessed and enjoyed in this life, if beyond it he sees, he wishes, he craves nothing more? Fortune and success, then, seem the essential condition for happiness, and they are the paramount cause of the envy that gnaws his heart. Only another illusion! Probably the most restless and discontented men to-day are those who have won success most easily and found fortune most benign. Every wish once gratified wears upon a man, and brings forth new wants, ever the more importunate. What before possession seemed enviable fortune, proves soon after the winning but the gray uniformity of a wonted condition: upon the height sighed for from afar, man walks as on a wearisome lowland plain. New aspirations are forever springing into being from aspirations satisfied; and if at a certain juncture a man does not manage to direct his mind toward some goal fixed beyond the term of his natural existence; if he does not find his joy in working for a prize unattainable as long as he lives, he will one day find himself full of riches and of discontent, fortuned materially, beggared in mind. No man—not even of the rarest intelligence and

189

energy—can satisfy desires, constantly self-renewing, in a world where every man is searching for some portion of felicity. And every man, after having secured his part of the good things of this life, is bound to withdraw himself to enjoy them in tranquillity and to leave the field free to those who have not yet acquired their share: if he be not disposed to make this renunciation spontaneously, other men almost invariably find the means to constrain him to it!

Full of worldly goods, but infelicitous, is the state of many a man whom the masses envy most. He seeks to shake off the plague of satisfied desires by running about the world, multiplying the diversions and excitements of his surroundings, straining his powers in frenzied labor that has no aim if not itself, nor can it further serve, unless to astound us: but in vain! The automobile cannot become a factor in felicity when the organ of felicity is atrophied within us. Machines can write, cut, saw, weigh, run, make accounts, and, in part, think for us; but they cannot solve the insoluble contradictions of our sensibility and our sentiment,

nor annul the effects of our selfishness. The
man who lives only in himself, for himself,
with himself, will torment himself to the end.
There is but one means adequate to hold in
check the insatiable eagerness of sense and
passion—that is, to desire intensely, with
faith, something outside ourselves, striving
energetically to win it. This means is at the
disposition of all, the poor as well as the
rich, the unlettered as well as the learned—
perhaps the poor and the ignorant can make
even readier and larger use of it than the
rich!

Herein subsists the true human equality;
that which is not written in statute laws,
nor is it proclaimed by formal religions, but
which exists in the individual human soul,
and in the laws that govern the passions and
the thoughts of man, eternal and immutable
as the physical laws of nature. How often
has man protested against that mysterious
force that scatters in so arbitrary a fashion,
with such apparent injustice, the material
and moral good things of life? Why has one
man a profound and brilliant genius, while
another's mind is simple and slow? Why

should some men have money, delight in art, enjoy luxury, command their fellows, while others live sadly, in poverty, in ignorance, subordinate to others? These protests would be legitimate and well founded if wealth and power were the absolute causes of satisfaction. They are, instead, often the occasions of unhappiness, of corruption, of *ennui*, exactly because a man rich and powerful, vainglorious, vitiated by facility in pleasure, almost invariably makes himself his own god, confounds the brief moment of his stay upon earth with eternity, and forgets how to wish for anything beyond time and self. All historians have been surprised at the moral degeneration that sooner or later undoes classes and families, once arrived at power and wealth,—that corruption and weakness which sooner or later supplant the virtues of the forefathers, who acquired the greatness. The main cause of this decadence is always the same: incapacity to will and to long for something beyond personal pleasure.

I know that many people regard this tendency of the modern mind to separate itself from all beliefs that set before man an un-temporal aim, as an effect of the intellectual progress and of the growing ability and culture of our age. All the forms through which men have sought to render comprehensible to the multitude the philosophical concept of the future life—what are they to them but children's fables, which the matured reason throws away, laughing? Why—they ask —in an age when personal energy is the might that moulds the world, must the ardor of the young stand subject to the prudence of the old, in family traditions that are the cult of decrepit nations? It seems to many that democratic progress has done great service to man in eradicating immortality from the heart, a plant at home only in the soil of prejudice and aristocratic injustice. But should not all men feel themselves more readily equals and brothers, since all are bound to disappear together forever, with their own time?

I would not press this theory to its limits, but merely maintain that it has a content of truth, like all theories on human affairs. Since the world to-day is more inclined to admire its virtues than to recognize its defects, I prefer to insist upon one point—asking, how far is this transformation of ideas and sentiments the effect of an overgrown egoism? It is so convenient—or at least at first sight it seems so convenient—to live only in the present, to spend all our efforts upon ourselves, to take into the account of real happiness only what can be seen, touched, numbered, weighed, measured! All civilizations decay from an excess of egoism, the product of wealth and power: are not these phenomena that we witness a proof that our boasted civilization also begins to suffer from this moral disease? With the growing indifference to the unseen world and the problems of the future life, is there not also diffused a dangerous indifference to the interests of the species?

In fact, as always happens, this egoism, once apparently wise, begins to prove itself ingenuous and fallacious. Pretending to insure to man more happiness than he can actually enjoy, it loads him with annoyance, with weariness and dissatisfaction. The moral restlessness that belonged in the past to a few *élites*, overrich, overlearned, and therefore self-centred, is now spread throughout two continents, in all classes, notwithstanding the ameliorated material conditions and the advance of culture. This is not strange, at least for him who knows men and history; since neither increased comfort nor wider instruction will further the happiness of man if it teaches him only to wear shinier shoes and better laundered collars, but gives him no mind to look before him beyond his own allotted lifetime.

HENRY   JAMES

Is There a Life After Death?

Henry James

IX

Is There a Life After Death?

PART I

I CONFESS at the outset that I think it the most interesting question in the world, once it takes on all the intensity of which it is capable. It does that, insidiously but inevitably, as we live longer and longer—does it at least for many persons; I myself, in any case, find it increasingly assert its power to attach and, if I may use the word so unjustly compromised by trivial applications, to amuse. I say "assert its power" so to occupy us, because I mean to express only its most general effect. That effect on our spirit is mostly either one of two forms; the effect of making us desire death, and for reasons, absolutely *as* welcome extinction and termination; or the effect of making us desire it as a renewal of the interest, the appreciation, the passion, the large and consecrated consciousness, in a word, of which we have had so splendid a sample in this world. Either one or the other of these opposed states of feeling is bound finally to declare itself, we judge, in persons of a fine sensibility and whose innermost spirit experience has set vibrating at all; for the condition of indifference and of knowing neither is the condition of living altogether so much below the human privilege as to have little right to pass for unjustly excluded or neglected in this business of the speculative reckoning.

That an immense number of persons should not recognize the appeal of our speculation, or even be aware of the existence of our question, is a fact that might seem to demand, in the whole connection, some particular consideration; but our anxiety, our hope, or our fear, hangs before us, after all, only because it more or less torments us, and in order to contribute in any degree to a discussion of the possibility we have to be consciously in presence of it. I can only see it, the great interrogation or the great deprecation we are ultimately driven to, as a part of our general concern with life and our general, and extremely various—because I speak of each man's general—mode of reaction under it; but to testify for an experience we must have reacted in one way or another. The weight of those who don't react may be felt, it it true, in one of the scales; for it may very well be asked on their behalf whether they are distinguishable as "living" either before or after. Only the special reaction of others, or the play of *their* speculation, however, will, in due consideration, have put it there. How *can* there be a personal and a differentiated life "after," it will then of course be asked, for those for whom there has been so little of one before?—unless indeed it be pronounced conceivable that the possibility may vary from man to man, from human case to human case, and that the quantity or the quality of our practice of consciousness may have something to say to it. If I myself am disposed to pronounce this conceivable—as verily I expect to find myself before we have done—I must glance at a few other relations of the matter first.

My point for the moment is that the more or less visibly diminishing distance which separates us at a certain age from death is, however we are affected toward the supposition of an existence beyond it, an intensifier of the feeling that most works in us, and that in the light of the lamp so held up our aggravated sense of life, as I may perhaps best call it, our impression of what we have been through, is what essentially fosters and determines, on the whole ground, our desire or our aversion. So, at any rate, the situation strikes me, and one can speak of it but for one's personal self. The subject is portentous and any individual utterance upon it, however ingenious or however grave, but comparatively a feeble pipe or a pathetic quaver; yet I hold that as we can scarce have too many visions, too many statements or pictures of the conceived social Utopia that the sincere fond dreamer, the believer in better things, may find glimmer before him, so the sincere and struggling son of earth among his fellow-strugglers reports of the positive or negative presumption in the savor of his world, that is not to be of earth, and thus drops his testimony, however scant, into the reservoir. It all depends, in other words, the weight or the force or the interest of this testimony does, on what life has predominantly said to us. And there are those—I take them for the constant and vast majority —to whom it in the way of intelligible suggestion says nothing. Possibly immortality itself—or another chance at least, as we may freely call it—will say as little; which is a fair and simple manner of disposing of the idea of a new start in relation to them. Though, indeed, I must add, the contemplative critic scarce—save under one probability—sees why the universe should be at the expense of a new start for those on whom the old start appears (though but to our purblind sight, it may, of course, be replied) so to have been wasted. The probability is, in fact, that what we dimly discern as waste the wisdom of the universe may know as a very different matter. We don't think of slugs and jellyfish as the waste, but rather as the amusement, the attestation of wealth and variety, of gardens and sea-beaches; so why should we, under stress, in respect to the human scene and its discussable sequel, think differently of dull people?

This is but an instance, or a trifle, however, among the difficulties with which the whole case bristles for those on whom the fact of the lived life has insisted on thrusting it, and which it yet leaves them tormentedly to deal with. The question is of the *personal* experience, of course, of another existence; of its being I my very self, and you, definitely, and he and she, who resume and go on, and not of unthinkable substitutes or metamorphoses. The whole interest of the matter is that it is my or your sensibility that is involved and at stake; the thing figuring to us as momentous just because that sensibility and its tasted fruits, as we owe them to life, are either remunerative enough and sweet enough or too barren and too bitter. Only because posthumous survival in some other conditions involves what we know, what we have enjoyed and suffered, as our particular personal adventure, does it appeal to us or excite our protest; only because of the *associations* of consciousness do we trouble and consult ourselves—do we wish the latter pro-

longed and wonder if it may not be indestructible, or decide that we have had enough
of it and invoke the conclusion that we have
so had it once for all. We pass, I think,
through many changes of impression, many
shifting estimates, as to the force and value
of those associations; and there is no single,
there is no decisive sense of them in which,
throughout our earthly course, it is easy or
needful to rest.

Whatever we may begin with we almost
inevitably go on, under the discipline of life,
to more or less. resigned acceptance of the
grim fact that "science" takes no account
of the soul, the principle we worry about, and
that, as however nobly thinking and feeling
creatures, we are abjectly and inveterately
shut up in our material organs. We flutter
away from that account of ourselves, on sublime occasion, only to come back to it with
the collapse of our wings, and during much
of our life the grim view, as I have called it,
the sense of the rigor of our physical basis,
is confirmed to us by overwhelming appearances. The mere spectacle, all about us, of
personal decay, and of the decay, as seems,

of the whole being, adds itself formidably to that of so much bloom and assurance and energy—the things we catch in the very fact of their material identity. There are times when *all* the elements and qualities that constitute the affirmation of the personal life here affect us as making against any apprehensible other affirmation of it. And that general observation and evidence abide with us and keep us company; they reinforce the verdict of the dismal laboratories and the confident analysts as to the interconvertibility of our genius, as it comparatively is at the worst, and our brain—the poor palpable, ponderable, probeable, laboratory - brain that we ourselves see in certain inevitable conditions —become as naught.

It brings itself home to us thus in all sorts of ways that we are even at our highest flights of personality, our furthest reachings out of the mind, of the very stuff of the abject actual, and that the sublimest idea we can form and the noblest hope and affection we can cherish are but flowers sprouting in that eminently and infinitely diggable soil. It may be as favorable to them—as well as to quite other moral growths—as we are free to note; but we see its power to put them forth break down and end, and ours to receive them from it to do the same—we watch the relentless ebb of the tide on which the vessel of experience carries us, and which to our earthly eyes never flows again. It is to the personality that the idea of renewed being attaches itself, and we see nothing so much written over the personalities of the world as that they are finite and precarious and insusceptible. All the ugliness, the grossness, the stupidity, the cruelty, the vast extent to which the score in question is a record of brutality and vulgarity, the so easy non-existence of consciousness, round about us as to most of the things that make for living desirably at all, or even for living once, let alone on the enlarged chance—these things fairly rub it into us that to *have* a personality need create no presumption beyond what this remarkably mixed world is by itself amply sufficient to meet. A renewal of being, we ask, for people who understand being, even here, where renewals, of sorts, are possible, that way, and that way, apparently, alone?—leaving us vainly to wonder, in presence of such obvious and offensive matter for decay and putrescence, what there is for renewal to take hold of, or what element may be supposed fine enough to create a claim for disengagement. The mere fact in short that so much of life as we know it dishonors, or at any rate falls below, the greater part of the beauty and the opportunity even of this world, works upon us for persuasion that none other can be eager to receive it.

With which all the while there co-operates the exhibited limitation of our faculty for persistence, for not giving way, for not doing more than attest the inextinguishable or extinguishable spark in the mere minimum of time. The thinkable, the possible, we are fairly moved to say, in the way of the resistances and renewals of our conceded day, baffle us and are already beyond our command; I mean in the sense that the spirit even still in activity never shows as recovering, before our present eyes, an inch of the ground the body has once fairly taken from it. The personality, the apparently final eclipse of which by death we are discussing, fails, we remark, of any partial victory over partial eclipses, and keeps before us, once for all, the same sharp edge of blackness on the compromised disk of light. Even while "we" nominally go on those parts of us that have been overdarkened become as dead; our extinct passions and faculties and interests, that is, refuse to revive; our personality, by which I mean our "soul," declining in many a case, or in most, by inches, is aware of itself at any given moment as it is, however contracted, and not as it *was*, however magnificent; we may die piecemeal, but by no sign ever demonstrably caught does the "liberated" spirit react from death piecemeal. The answer to that may of course be that such reactions as can be "caught" are not claimed for it even by the fondest lovers of the precarious idea; the most that is claimed is that the reaction takes place *somewhere*—and the farther away from the conditions and circumstances of death the more probably. The apparently significant thing is none the less that during slow and successive stages of material extinction *some* nearness—of the personal quantity departing to

209

the personal quantity remaining, and in the
name of personal association and personal
affection, and to the abatement of utter personal eclipse—might be supposable; and
that this is what we miss.

Such, at least, is one of the faces, however
small, that life put on to persuade us of the
utterly contingent nature of our familiar inward ease—ease of being—and that, to our
comfort or our disconcertment, this familiarity is a perfectly restricted thing. And
so we go on noting, through our time and
amid the abundance of life, everything that
makes, to our earthly senses, for the unmistakable absoluteness of death. Every hour
affords us some fresh illustration of it, drawn
especially from the condition of others; but
one, if we really heed it, recurs and recurs
as the most poignant of all. How can we
not make much of the terrible fashion in
which the universe takes upon itself to em-
phasize and multiply the disconnectedness of
those who vanish from our sight?—or they
perhaps not so much from ours as we from
theirs; though indeed if once we lend ourselves to the hypothesis of posthumous reno-

vation at all, the fact that our ex-fellow-mortals would appear thus to have taken up some very much better interest than the poor world they have left might pass for a positively favorable argument. On the basis of their enjoying another state of being, we have certainly to assume that this is the case, for to the probability of a quite different case the inveteracy of their neglect of the previous one, through all the ages and the spaces, the grimness of their utter refusal, so far as we know it, of a retrospective personal sign, would seem directly to point. (I can only treat here as absolutely not established the value of those personal signs that ostensibly come to us through the trance medium. These often make, I grant, for attention and wonder and interest—but for interest above all in the medium and the trance. Whether or no they may in the given case seem to savor of another state of being on the part of those from whom they profess to come, they savor intensely, to my sense, of the medium and the trance, and, with their remarkable felicities and fitnesses, their immense call for explanation, invest that personage, in that state, with an almost irresistible attraction.)

Here it is, at any rate, that we break ourselves against that conception of immortality *as* personal which is the only thing that gives it meaning or relevance. That it shall be personal and yet shall so entirely and relentlessly have yielded to dissociation, this makes us ask if such terms for it are acceptable to thought. Is to be as dissociated as that consistent with personality as we understand *our* share in the condition?—since on any contingency save *by* that understanding of it our interest in the subject drops. I practically know what I am talking about when I say, "I," hypothetically, for my full experience of another term of being, just as I know it when I say "I" for my experience of this one; but I shouldn't in the least do so were I not *able* to say "I"—had I to reckon, that is, with a failure of the signs by which I know myself. In presence of the great question I cling to these signs more than ever, and to conceive of the actual achievement of immortality by others who may have had like knowledge I have to impute to such others a clinging to similar signs. Yet with that advantage, as it were, for any friendly re-participation, whether for our sake or for their own, in that consciousness in which they bathed themselves on earth, they yet appear to find no grain of relief to bestow on our anxiety, no dimmest spark to flash upon our ignorance. This fact, as after middle life we continue to note it, contributes to the confirmation, within us, of our seeming aware-ness of extinct things *as* utterly and veritably extinct, with whatever splendid intensity we may have known them to live; an awareness that settles upon us with a formidable weight as time and the world pile up around us all their affirmation of *other* things, and all im-portunate ones—which little by little acts upon us as so much triumphant negation of the past and the lost; the flicker of some vast sardonic, leering "Don't you see?" on the mask of Nature.

We tend so to feel *that* become for us the last word on the matter that all Nature and all life and all society and all so-called knowl-edge, with everything these huge, grim in-differences strive to make, and to some degree succeed in making, of ourselves, take the form and have the effect of a mass of machinery for ignoring and denying, the universe through, everything that is not of their own actuality. So it is, therefore, that we keep on and that we reflect; we begin by pitying the remembered dead, even for the very danger of our indifference to them, and we end by pitying ourselves for the final demonstration, as it were, of their indifference to us. "They must be dead, indeed," we say; "they must be as dead as 'science' affirms, for this consecration of it on such a scale, and with these tremendous rites of nullification, to take place." We think of the particular cases of those who could have been backed, as we call it, not to fail, on occasion, of somehow reaching us. We recall the forces of passion, of reason, of personality, that lived in them, and what such forces had made them, to our sight, capable of; and then we say, conclusively, "Talk of triumphant identity if *they*, wanting to triumph, haven't done it!"

Those in whom we saw consciousness, to all appearance, the consciousness of *us*, slowly *déménager*, piece by piece, so that they more or less consentingly parted with it—of *them* let us take it, under stress, if we must, that their ground for interest (in us and in other matters) "unmistakably" reached its limit. But what of those lights that went out in a single gust and those life passions that were nipped in their flower and their promise? Are these spirits thinkable as having emptied the measure the services of sense could offer them? Do we feel capable of a brutal rupture with registered promises, started curiosities, waiting initiations? The mere acquired momentum of intelligence, of perception, of vibration, of experience in a word, would have carried them on, we argue, to *something*, the something that never takes place for us, if the laboratory-brain were *not* really all. What it comes to is then that our faith or our hope may to some degree resist the fact, once accomplished, of watched and deplored death, but that they may well break down before the avidity and consistency with which everything insufferably *continues* to die.

PART II

I have said "we argue" as we take in impressions of the order of those I have glanced at and of which I have pretended to mention only a few. I am not, however, putting them forward for their direct weight in the scale; I speak of them but as the inevitable obsession of those who with the failure of the illusions of youth have had to learn more and more to reckon with reality. For if I referred previously to their bearing us increase of company I mean this to be true with the qualification that applies to our whole attitude, or that of many of us, on our question —the fact that it is subject to the very shifting admonitions of that reality, which may seem to us at times to mean one thing and at times quite another. Yet rather than attempt to speak, to this effect, even for "many of us," I had best do so simply for myself, since it is only for one's self that one can positively answer. It is a matter of individual experience, which I have seen multiply, to satiety, the obsessions I have named and then

suffer them to be displaced by others—only
once more to reappear again and once more
to give way. I speak as one who has had
time to take many notes, to be struck with
many differences, and to see, a little typically
perhaps, what may eventually happen; and
I contribute thus, and thus only, my grain of
consideration to the store.

I began, I may accordingly say, with a
distinct sense that our question didn't appeal to me—as it appeals, in general, but
scantly to the young—and I was content for
a long time to let it alone, only asking that
it should, in turn, as irrelevant and insoluble,
let *me*. This it did, in abundance, for many
a day—which is, however, but another way
of saying that death remained for me, in a
large measure, unexhibited and unaggressive.
The exhibition, the aggression of life was
quite ready to cover the ground and fill the
bill, and to my sense of that balance still inclined even after the opposite pressure had
begun to show in the scale. Resented bereavement is all at first—and may long go
on appearing more than anything else—one
of the exhibitions of life; the various forms

and necessities of our resentment sufficiently meet then the questions that death brings up. That aspect changes, however, as we seem to see what it is to die—and to have died—in contradistinction to suffering (which means to warmly *being*) on earth; and as we so see what it is the difficulties involved in the thought of its not being absolute tend to take possession of us and rule us. Treating my own case, again, as a "given" one, I found it long impossible not to succumb—so far as one began to yield at all to irresistible wonder—to discouragement by the mere pitiless dryness of all the appearances. This was for years quite blighting to my sensibility; and the appearances, as I have called them—and as they make, in "science" particularly, the most assured show—imposed themselves; the universe, or all of it that I could make out, kept proclaiming in a myriad voices that I and my poor form of consciousness were a quantity it could at any moment perfectly do without, even in what I might be pleased to call our very finest principle. If without me then just so without others; all the more that if it was not so dispensing with them the simply *bête* situation of one's forever and forever failing of the least whiff of a positive symptom to the contrary would not so ineffably persist.

During which period, none the less, as I was afterward to find, the question subtly took care of itself for me—waking up as I did gradually, in the event (very slowly indeed, with no sudden start of perception, no bound of enthusiasm), to its facing me with a "mild but firm" refusal to regard itself as settled. That circumstance once noted, I began to inquire—mainly, I confess, of myself—why it should be thus obstinate, what reason it could at all clearly give me; and this led me in due course to my getting, or at least framing my reply: a reply not perhaps so multitudinous as those voices of the universe that I have spoken of as discouraging, but which none the less, I find, still holds its ground for me. What had happened, in short, was that all the while I had been practically, though however dimly, trying to take the measure of my consciousness—on this appropriate and prescribed basis of its being so finite—I had learned, as I may say, to live in it more, and with the consequence of thereby not a little undermining the conclusion most unfavorable to it. I had doubtless taken thus to increased living in it by reaction against so grossly finite a world—for it at least *contained* the world, and could handle and criticise it, could play with it and deride it; it had *that* superiority: which meant, all the while, such successful living that the abode itself grew more and more interesting to me, and with this beautiful sign of its character that the more and the more one asked of it the more and the more it appeared to give. I should perhaps rather say that the more one turned it, as an easy reflector, here and there and everywhere over the immensity of things, the more it appeared to take; which is but another way of putting, for "interest," the same truth.

I recognize that the questions I have come after this fashion to ask my consciousness are questions embarrassed by the conditions of this world; but it has none the less left me at last with a sense that, beautiful and adorable thing, it is capable of sorts of action for which I have not as yet even the wit to call upon it. Of what I suggestively find in it, at any rate, I shall speak; but I must first explain the felt connection between this enlarged impression of its quality and *portée* and the improved discussibility of a life hereafter. I hope, then, I shall not seem to push the relation of that idea to the ampler enjoyment of consciousness beyond what it will bear when I say that the ground is gained by the great extension so obtained for one's precious inward "personality"—one's personality not at all in itself of course, or on its claims of general importance, but as conceivably hanging together for survival. It is not that I have found in growing older any one marked or momentous line in the life of the mind or in the play and the freedom of the imagination to be stepped over; but that a process takes place which I can only describe as the accumulation of the very treasure itself of consciousness. I won't say that "the world," as we commonly refer to it, grows more attaching, but will say that the universe increasingly does, and that this makes us present at the enormous multiplication of our possible relations with it; relations still vague, no doubt, as undefined as they are uplifting, as they are inspiring, to think of, and on a scale beyond our actual use or application, yet filling us (through the "law" in question, the law that consciousness gives us immensities and imaginabilities wherever we direct it) with the unlimited vision of being. This mere fact that so small a part of one's visionary and speculative and emotional activity has even a traceably indirect bearing on one's doings or purposes or particular desires contribute strangely to the luxury—which is the magnificent waste—of thought, and strongly reminds one that even should one cease to be in love with life it would be difficult, on such terms, not to be in love with living.

Living, or feeling one's exquisite curiosity about the universe fed and fed, rewarded and rewarded—though I of course don't say definitely answered and answered—becomes thus the highest good I can conceive of, a million times better than not living (however *that* comfort may at bad moments have solicited us); all of which illustrates what I mean by the consecrated "interest" of con-

sciousness. It so peoples and animates and
extends and transforms itself; it so gives me
the chance to take, on behalf of my personality, these inordinate intellectual and ir-
responsible liberties with the idea of things.
And, once more—speaking for myself only
and keeping to the facts of my experience—
it is above all as an artist that I appreciate
this beautiful and enjoyable independence
of thought and more especially this assault
of the boundlessly multiplied personal relation (my own), which carries me beyond
even any "profoundest" observation of this
world whatever, and any mortal adventure,
and refers me to realizations I am condemned
as yet but to dream of. For the artist the
sense of our luxurious "waste" of postulation
and supposition is of the strongest; of him
is it superlatively true that he knows the
aggression as of infinite numbers of modes
of being. His case, as I see it, is easily such
as to make him declare that if he were not
constantly, in his commonest processes, carrying the field of consciousness further and
further, making it lose itself in the ineffable,
he shouldn't in the least feel himself an

artist. As more or less of one myself, for instance, I deal with being, I invoke and evoke, I figure and represent, I seize and fix, as many phases and aspects and conceptions of it as my infirm hand allows me strength for; and in so doing I find myself—I can't express it otherwise—in communication with *sources;* sources to which I owe the apprehension of far more and far other combinations than observation and experience, in their ordinary sense, have given me the pattern of.

The truth is that to live, to this tune, intellectually, and in order to do beautiful things, with questions of being as such questions may for the man of imagination aboundingly come up, is to find one's view of one's share in it, and above all of its appeal to *be* shared, in an infinite variety, enormously enlarged. The very provocation offered to the artist by the universe, the provocation to him to *be*—poor man who may know so little what he's in for!—an artist, and thereby supremely serve it; what do I take that for but the intense desire of being to get itself personally shared, to show itself for personally sharable, and thus foster the sublimest faith? If the artist's surrender to invasive floods is accordingly nine-tenths of the matter that makes his consciousness, that makes mine, so persuasively interesting, so I should see people of our character peculiarly victimized if the vulgar arrangement of our fate, as I have called it, imputable to the power that produced us, should prove to be the true one. For I think of myself as enjoying the very maximum reason to desire the renewal of existence—existence the forms of which I have had admirably and endlessly to *cultivate*—and as therefore embracing it in thought as a possible something that shall be better than what we have known here; only then to ask myself if it be credible that the power just mentioned is simply enjoying the unholy "treat" or brutal amusement of encouraging that conviction in us in order to say with elation: "Then you shall have it, the charming confidence (for I shall wantonly let it come to that), only so long as that it shall beautifully mature; after which, as soon as the prospect has vividly and desirably opened out to you, you shall become as naught."

225

"Well, you *will* have had them, the sense
and the vision of existence," the rejoinder
on that may be; to which I retort in turn:
"Yes, I shall have them exactly for the space
of time during which the question of my
appetite for what they represent may clear
itself up. The complete privation, as a more
or less prompt sequel to that clearance, is
worthy but of the wit of a sniggering little
boy who makes his dog jump at a morsel only
to whisk it away; a practical joke of the
lowest description, with the execrable taste of
which I decline to charge our prime origi-
nator."

I do not deny of course that the case may
be different for those who have had another
experience—there are so many different experiences of consciousness possible, and with
the result of so many different positions on
the matter. Those to whom such dreadful
things have happened that they haven't even
the refuge of the negative state of mind, but
have been driven into the exasperated positive, so that they but long to lay down the
burden of being and never again take it up—
these unfortunates have an equal chance of

expressing their attitude and of making it as eloquent and as representative as they will. Their testimony may easily be tremendous and their revelation black. Will they belong, however, to the class of those the really main condition of whose life is to work and work their inner spirit to a productive or illustrative end, and so to feel themselves find in it a general warrant for anything and everything, in the way of particular projections and adventures, that they may dream that spirit susceptible of? This comes again to asking, doubtless, whether it has been their fate to perceive themselves, in the fulness of time, and for good or for ill, living preponderantly by the imagination and having to call upon it at every turn to see them through. By which I don't mean to say that no sincere artist has ever been overwhelmed by life and found his connections with the infinite cut, so that his history may *seem* to represent for him so much evidence that this so easily awful world is the last word to us, and a horrible one at that: cases confounding me could quite too promptly be adduced. The point is, none the less, that in proportion as we (of the class I speak of) enjoy the greater number of our most characteristic inward reactions, in proportion as we do curiously and lovingly, yearningly and irrepressibly, interrogate and liberate, try and test and explore, our general productive and, as we like conveniently to say, creative awareness of things—though the individual, I grant, may pull his job off on occasion and for a while and yet never have done so at all —in that proportion does our function strike us as establishing sublime relations. It is this effect of working it that is exquisite, it is the character of the response it makes, and the merest fraction or dimmest shade of which is ever reported again in what we "have to show"; it is in a word the artistic consciousness and privilege in itself that thus shines as from immersion in the fountain of being. Into that fountain, to depths immeasurable, our spirit dips—to the effect of feeling itself, *quâ* imagination and aspiration, all scented with universal sources. What is that but an adventure of our personality, and how can we after it hold complete disconnection likely?

I do not so hold it, I profess, for my own part, and, above all, I freely concede, do not in the least want to. Consciousness has thus arrived at interesting me too much and on too great a scale—that is all my revelation or my secret; on too great a scale, that is, for me not to ask myself what she can mean by such blandishments—to the altogether normally hampered and benighted random individual that I am. Does she mean nothing more than that I shall have found life, by her enrichment, the more amusing here? But I find it, at this well-nigh final pass, mainly amusing in the light of the possibility that the idea of an exclusively present world, with all its appearances wholly dependent on our physical outfit, may represent for us but a chance for experiment in the very interest of our better and freer being and to its very honor and reinforcement; but a chance for the practice and initial confidence of our faculties and our passions, of the precious personality at stake—precious to *us* at least—which shall have been not unlike the sustaining frame on little wheels that often encases growing infants, so that, dangling and shaking about in it, they may feel their assurance of walking increase and teach their small toes to know the ground. I like to think that we here, as to soul, dangle from the infinite and shake about in the universe; that this world and this conformation and these senses are our helpful and ingenious frame, amply provided with wheels and replete with the lesson for us of how to plant, spiritually, our feet. That conception of the matter rather comes back, I recognize, to the theory of the spiritual discipline, the purification and preparation on earth for heaven, of the orthodox theology—which is a resemblance I don't object to, all the more that it is a superficial one, as well as a fact mainly showing, at any rate, how neatly extremes may sometimes meet.

My mind, however that may be, doesn't in the least resent its association with all the highly appreciable and perishable matter of which the rest of my personality is composed; nor does it fail to recognize the beautiful assistance—alternating indeed frequently with the extreme inconvenience—received from it; representing, as these latter forms do, much ministration to experience. The ministration may have sometimes affected my consciousness as clumsy, but has at other times affected it as exquisite, and it accepts and appropriates and consumes everything the universe puts in its way; matter in tons, if necessary, so long as such quantities are, in so mysterious and complicated a sphere, one of its conditions of activity. Above all, it takes kindly to that admirable philosophic view which makes of matter the mere encasement or sheath, thicker, thinner, coarser, finer, more transparent or more obstructive, of a spirit it has no more concern in producing than the baby-frame has in producing the intelligence of the baby—much as that intelligence may be so promoted.

I "like" to think, I may be held too artlessly to repeat, that this, that, and the other appearances are favorable to the idea of the independence, behind everything (*its* everything), of my individual soul; I "like" to think even at the risk of lumping myself with those shallow minds who are happily and foolishly able to believe what they would prefer. It isn't really a question of belief—

which is a term I have made no use of in these remarks; it is on the other hand a question of desire, but of desire so confirmed, so thoroughly established and nourished, as to leave belief a comparatively irrelevant affair. There is one light, moreover, under which they come to the same thing—at least in presence of a question as insoluble as the one before us. If one acts from desire quite as one would from belief, it signifies little what name one gives to one's motive. By which term action I mean action of the mind, mean that I can encourage my consciousness to acquire that interest, to live in that elasticity and that affluence, which affect me as symptomatic and auspicious. I can't do less if I desire, but I shouldn't be able to do more if I believed. Just so I shouldn't be able to do more than cultivate belief; and it is exactly to cultivation that I subject my hopeful sense of the auspicious; with such success—or at least with such intensity—as to give me the splendid illusion of doing something myself for my prospect, or at all events for my own possibility, of immortality. There again, I recognize extremes "neatly meet";

one doesn't talk otherwise, doubtless, of one's
working out one's salvation. But this coin-
cidence too I am perfectly free to welcome—
putting it, that is, that the theological pro-
vision happens to coincide with (or, for all I
know, to have been, at bottom, insidiously
built on) some such sense of appearances as
my own. If I am talking, at all events, of
what I "like" to think I may, in short, say
all: I like to think it open to me to establish
speculative and imaginative connections, to
take up conceived presumptions and pledges,
that have for me all the air of not being de-
cently able to escape redeeming themselves.
And when once such a mental relation to the
question as that begins to hover and settle,
who shall say over what fields of experience,
past and current, and what immensities of
perception and yearning, it shall *not* spread
the protection of its wings? No, no, no—I
reach beyond the laboratory-brain.

THE END

THE LITERATURE OF
DEATH AND DYING

Abrahamsson, Hans. **The Origin of Death:** Studies in African Mythology. 1951

Alden, Timothy. **A Collection of American Epitaphs and Inscriptions with Occasional Notes.** Five vols. in two. 1814

Austin, Mary. **Experiences Facing Death.** 1931

Bacon, Francis. **The Historie of Life and Death with Observations Naturall and Experimentall for the Prolongation of Life.** 1638

Barth, Karl. **The Resurrection of the Dead.** 1933

Bataille, Georges. **Death and Sensuality:** A Study of Eroticism and the Taboo. 1962

Bichat, [Marie François] Xavier. **Physiological Researches on Life and Death.** 1827

Browne, Thomas. **Hydriotaphia.** 1927

Carrington, Hereward. **Death:** Its Causes and Phenomena with Special Reference to Immortality. 1921

Comper, Frances M. M., editor. **The Book of the Craft of Dying and Other Early English Tracts Concerning Death.** 1917

Death and the Visual Arts. 1976

Death as a Speculative Theme in Religious, Scientific, and Social Thought. 1976

Donne, John. **Biathanatos.** 1930

Farber, Maurice L. **Theory of Suicide.** 1968

Fechner, Gustav Theodor. **The Little Book of Life After Death.** 1904

Frazer, James George. **The Fear of the Dead in Primitive Religion.** Three vols. in one. 1933/1934/1936

Fulton, Robert. **A Bibliography on Death, Grief and Bereavement:** 1845-1975. 1976

Gorer, Geoffrey. **Death, Grief, and Mourning.** 1965

Gruman, Gerald J. **A History of Ideas About the Prolongation of Life.** 1966

Henry, Andrew F. and James F. Short, Jr. **Suicide and Homicide.** 1954

Howells, W[illiam] D[ean], et al. **In After Days;** Thoughts on the Future Life. 1910

Irion, Paul E. **The Funeral:** Vestige or Value? 1966

Landsberg, Paul-Louis. **The Experience of Death:** The Moral Problem of Suicide. 1953

Maeterlinck, Maurice. **Before the Great Silence.** 1937

Maeterlinck, Maurice. **Death.** 1912

Metchnikoff, Élie. **The Nature of Man:** Studies in Optimistic Philosophy. 1910

Metchnikoff, Élie. **The Prolongation of Life:** Optimistic Studies. 1908

Munk, William. **Euthanasia.** 1887

Osler, William. **Science and Immortality.** 1904

Return to Life: Two Imaginings of the Lazarus Theme. 1976

Stephens, C[harles] A[sbury]. **Natural Salvation:** The Message of Science. 1905

Sulzberger, Cyrus. **My Brother Death.** 1961

Taylor, Jeremy. **The Rule and Exercises of Holy Dying.** 1819

Walker, G[eorge] A[lfred]. **Gatherings from Graveyards.** 1839

Warthin, Aldred Scott. **The Physician of the Dance of Death.** 1931

Whiter, Walter. **Dissertation on the Disorder of Death.** 1819

Whyte, Florence. **The Dance of Death in Spain and Catalonia.** 1931

Wolfenstein, Martha. **Disaster:** A Psychological Essay. 1957

Worcester, Alfred. **The Care of the Aged, the Dying, and the Dead.** 1950

Zandee, J[an]. **Death as an Enemy According to Ancient Egyptian Conceptions.** 1960